Choose only Love

Wisdom

BOOK IV

Messages from A Choir of Angels
Received by Sebastián Blaksley

TAKE HEART PUBLICATIONS

Elige solo el amor | Choose Only Love

Publication in English authorized by
Fundación amor vivo, a nonprofit organization, Argentina
Av. Libertador 16434
San Isidro
Buenos Aires, Argentina
www.fundacionamorvivo.org,

TAKE HEART PUBLICATIONS
13315 Buttermilk Bend
North San Juan, CA 95960
www.takeheartpublications.com
ISBN 978-1-58469-685-8
Cover and editorial design by Alejandro Arrojo
Computer production by
Patty Arnold, *Menagerie Design and Publishing*
Manufactured in the United States of America
November, 2020

Choose only Love

Wisdom

Table of contents

How It Originated

On October 3, 2018, a presence that was all love and whose magnificence, beauty, and benevolence cannot be described, came to me suddenly in a way I had never before experienced. I understood with perfect clarity that it was the glorious Archangel Raphael. He introduced himself saying, "I am the medicine of God." He told me to pray a particular prayer for nine days. Through inner inspiration he also dictated certain intentions for me to pray. The prayers consisted of five Our Fathers, five Hail Marys, and five Glories, just as these prayers are presented in the Catholic Church, to which I belong.

On October 13, the day after finishing this novena of prayer, I began to receive glorious visits from a choir of countless angels of God accompanied by Archangel Raphael and Archangel Gabriel. Their love and beauty were indescribable. Through the choir came the Voice of Christ, expressed in an ineffable form and as images, shown in symbols visible to the spirit. I put the meaning of these images into written words, then voice recordings.

Each visitation was the same: First I received the images and heard the music that the choir presents, then the chorus departed but Archangels Raphael and Gabriel remained as custodians, or loving presences, until the message or session in question was transcribed.

The glorious Archangel Raphael is the one who guided me in the transcription, assuring that the message is properly received and that what was shown can be passed from image to word. Archangel Gabriel is the loving custodian of everything that concerns the work, not only in reference to the manifestation itself and to the writings, but to everything that arises and will arise from them.

The messages, or sessions, are shown to me as a picture of great beauty in which each form (which has no form) is in itself a voice, a "sound-image." What I hear is like the rhythmical twanging of a harp that becomes translated into words. This tune is a vibration of celestial music whose frequency is unlike the sounds of the world. It is a kind of "vibration-frequency" that the soul knows perfectly well and that I recognize with certainty as the voice of the Lamb of God. Once everything is transcribed in written and spoken words, then the chorus arrives in all its glory once again, as if they were coming to seek the most holy Archangels Raphael and Gabriel. Then all together they retire, singing a hosanna to the Christ of God.

That hosanna sung by the choir of angels is a majestic song of praise and gratitude to the Creator for the infinite mystery of love that is the second coming of Christ. It is a prelude to His coming. If humankind were able to understand in all its magnitude the ineffable mystery of love that is the Second Coming of Christ, we would eternally sing the mercies of God in union with all the angels.

In cases where the Mother Mary Herself or Jesus Christ are present in Their human and divine person and communicate directly, the choir of angels is muted with love, in a silence that is sacred. Pure expectation, so to speak, surrounds their blessed presences. The angels bow their heads, cast their eyes downward, and are caught up in an ecstasy of love, veneration, and contemplation. Nothing and no one dares, nor could, interrupt the holy silence in which the universe is submerged before the sovereign presence of Mary and Jesus when They speak directly to our souls. This is because that space of dialogue between Christ and the soul is inviolable. It is the sacred temple of the intimacy of the soul with God.

When Archangel Raphael makes himself present to me and begins the process of translating images and symbols into written words, my will is fused into one will with Him. We are one and the same will. There is no "you" and "me." And yet, even in that unity, there is the consciousness that I am I, and He is He: two persons with the same will, the same consciousness of being, in a single holy purpose. The thinking mind is silenced in this absorption of my being into the Being of all true being, which we share as a unit. My consciousness and His become one. What the will one says to be done, is done. There is no distance between the "be done" and its effect.

The rest of my humanity responds humbly. There is no resistance. There is only a flow of words coming from the Mind of Christ, as if it were from a spring that flows from the top of a mountain. It is this torrent of Grace made into words move the hands with speed and precision that far surpasses those experienced in what could be called my ordinary writing. The soul remains ecstatic with love and with a single desire—to remain forever fused with the beloved Christ, being of our being and of all true being.

During the visitations my whole being is bathed in great peace and joy, like being embraced by universal love. But after the concentration of putting the message into words, the body shows great fatigue. It seems that it is difficult for it to sustain the energy I receive. The part of the manifestation that includes the chorus of angels, the voice, and the images is something that can happen at any time, place, or in any circumstance. However, the transcription of the symbols received into written words and then spoken and recorded can be delayed until I can make myself available to do so. It may be immediately afterwards or several days later.

The main message of this work could be summarized as follows: The time for a new humanity has arrived, a humanity that is ready to manifest the living Christ in each of us. We are, each of us, Christ. This is the truth about us, even if we perceive ourselves differently. We are already prepared to be able to live life in the certainty that says: I no longer live, but it is Christ who lives in me. Helping us to realize this truth in our lives, here and now, is what this manifestation is about. All of Heaven will help us in this holy purpose, since it is the second Advent itself.

A Description of the Manifestations

When the Archangels come, they come without wings. They are like humans wearing tunics. Raphael's tunic is green, edged with gold. Gabriel's tunic is pink, almost white, edged with yellow. Both tunics are majestic, appearing as if made of a very precious silk.

Their faces are cheerful and radiant, with very light yellowish skin. Both have shoulder-length, golden blond hair and their eyes are green. They each have unique facial features. Their bodies are radiant with serene glowing light that generates peace and a great sense of beauty and harmony.

Many of the angels in the Chorus of Angels have light pink and light blue tunics. Others have light gold, but all are in pastel colors, again with a serene luminosity. A few have green robes as if they were emeralds but a little lighter.

The permanent happiness that angels exhibit is remarkable. Everything is joy with them. One day they told me that they radiate perpetual happiness because they always share happiness.

The angels are always surrounded by white and majestic light, as if they live in an eternal midday of love and light. They are accompanied by music, as though a celestial choir is singing in all corners of the universe, like the sound of millions of harps playing in unison, forming a harmonious symphony of great beauty.

The angelic vibrations are of such a degree that they calm the mind and the heart, and give peace. One knows, without knowing how, that this vibration is simultaneously prayer and praise. Each part of the universe (creation) sings a song of gratitude for it having been called into existence, as though it has music inside that is a prayer to the Creator. The soul had stopped hearing this celestial music but will begin to hear it again when it returns to the Father's house. Though forgotten, this song is forever loved by souls that love the Father and Creator.

The ineffable, inexpressible beauty of these visions of angels and archangels, submerges the soul in an ecstasy of love and rapture in which one's whole being participates. No joy or happiness on Earth compares with the ecstasy that a vision of the greatness, magnanimity, and beauty of the angels and archangels generates.

Angelic intelligence is of such a degree that it surpasses all worldly understanding. Their thoughts occur at an indescribable speed, even faster than human thought. Without distortion of any kind, their thoughts are pure without contradiction, with perfect clarity and express only holiness. As lightning crosses the firmament, so too do angelic thoughts pass through my mind.

I clearly perceive the difference between human thought and thought from the Wisdom of Heaven, due to the way I experience them. Thoughts from Heaven feel like light and breath; they are full of certainty, can never be forgotten, and bring a great "amount" of truth in the blink of an eye. In an instant I understand the full meaning of each manifestation that comes to me.

Humility, prudence, and simplicity are central features of the angels. Their greatest joy is to serve God by being servants of all creation. They love human beings, animals, plants, stones, the elements, and every material and immaterial aspect of creation with a love and tenderness that, when experienced, is capable of melting even the hardest heart.

While the beauty and magnanimity of angelic visions are indescribable, they are a pale flash compared to the magnificence of those of Jesus and Mary. Nothing in the universe resembles the eternal, unnameable beauty of the hearts of Jesus and Mary. They are God Himself made man and woman. They are the joy of the angels and have the veneration of creation. From Them springs all harmony, greatness, and holiness.

The looks of Jesus and Mary, radiating such tenderness and love, melt the entire universe. Their smiles are purity itself. In Their presence the soul is entranced in an ecstasy of veneration and contemplation, leaving it speechless. The soul exhales a moan of joy that says something like Ah! For me personally, contemplating the looks and smiles of Jesus and Mary is Heaven.

I hope you can understand what I'm trying to say as I try to describe the indescribable. I only say what I see, hear, and experience. Heaven exists, God exists, and God is love. This is what was given to me to see, hear, and understand.

I hope with all my heart that those who receive this manifestation let themselves be the beloved of God, more and more every day; and in this way be transformed by the beauty of a love that has no beginning or end.

With love in Christ,

Sebastian Blaksley,
A Soul in Love
Buenos Aires, Argentina
January, 2019 and October, 2020

Prelude

A message from Archangel Raphael

Beloveds of Heaven,

How much joy there is today in all creation! It is the joy we all share when we unite with you.

Oh humanity! If you had but an idea of how blessed are these dialogues of Divine Love, and how much we love those who live in the light of the living Christ, you would cry of happiness.

I am Archangel Raphael. I have come by divine design to serve. I thank you all, including you, the scribe from Heaven, for allowing me to collaborate in your lives.

I have come into your presence to give shape, in union and relationship, to this fourth book of this miraculous work. Through it, wisdom extends to the whole world, uniting in spirit and truth with all that is holy, beautiful, and perfect.

Before beginning the various sessions of this book, I would like to remind you that you are worthy children of God. Your dignity is such that a word cannot be conceived in your language that could express the greatness of your self. You are beloved children of God. You are redeemed humanity, perfect expressions of divine mercy. What one day was, is no longer, because it has never truly been. Now the new becomes reality in your self. You are the new humanity reborn in Christ.

My friends! Remember that I am closer to you than your own breath. I will always be by your side because you and I are one. In our equality lies the truth of who we are; I am not superior to you, nor to anyone.

In the realm of love there is no such thing as superiority or inferiority. No idea of separation is true. What I am is part of you, you are part of me, and we all are part of the Christ of God. We are creation, extending. We are unity of self.

1.

The All in All

A message from the Voice of Christ through a Choir of Angels, in the presence of Archangel Raphael and Archangel Gabriel

I. Prelude

Light of the world!
Come, extend your hand and take mine. Let us walk this path together. United, we dive deeper and deeper into the ocean of boundless wisdom that the truth is.

Reality contains within itself the mystery of God. Neither your eyes nor your other bodily senses can see it truly. Reality is a divine creation. Reality encompasses all the glory, splendor, and holiness that God is. All of it is what you are.

I would like to take you—and those who love the truth— back to the state in which you once lived within the unity of the being that is God. In that state the peace of Christ and you are one. In that state, in the mind of Christ, you are one with God and with all creation.

I am asking you to join me in the holy purpose of returning to the womb of the Divine Mother. God is Mother.

Until now, God Himself, in His infinite knowledge, wanted to show Himself in the world as Father, as well as the love that He is. But from now on She wants to show Herself as Mother, not only as wisdom. The "feminine" of God will come to light more and more every day. Indeed, it is already manifesting itself in an evident way.

Beloved brothers and sisters, just as the mind of God created the God-Father through Jesus of Nazareth, today He wants to create the dimension of Divine Mother. Mary is your example and perfect companion for this purpose as the incarnation of the Motherhood of God.

Mary is every woman, all Christ. Mary is the Woman-God, just as Jesus is the Man-God. While in each of them resides the whole, it is important that you consider that everything, for you, lives in the union of both.

II. Duality

Given the duality that exists in the world, in which the masculine has often overshadowed the feminine, today we begin to equalize both polarities in order to transcend them. This inner journey through which we go is the final part of the path towards restoration of your unique spiritual and physical memory of the self.

Returning unity to your memory will allow you to live consistently within it.

Unity, which is what you really are, has been seen as an external state to be reached. You have not yet come to abide in it consciously every day, even though the unity of the self is the truth about you.

To remain consciously in the radiant light of truth, that is, in the Heart of God, is that of which we speak. It is for this reason that this work has been conceived in the bosom of the Divine Mother, in the Immaculate Heart of Mary, in the very heart of love, to make possible the transcendence of opposites. To accomplish this transcendence of duality, it is important not to continue associating God or spirituality only with the masculine.

When Jesus created the God-Father, He was fully aware that humanity could only understand and accept a male God associated with authority, while including sonship and love. The idea of a Divine Father was perfect to introduce a God of love, who at the same time is also the Source of creation and thus the supreme authority without nullifying tenderness. It was necessary not to dissociate love from authority and divine strength. Only a creation of God-Father could do that within the consciousness of the time.

A God of love was a revolutionary idea two thousand years ago, and still is. The idea of a female God simply would not have been accepted. Humanity was not prepared for such an association with the feminine, much less with Oneness.

Christ Consciousness always includes human reality, and does not rush nor skip any process. The truth does not overlook any aspect of humanity, but integrates and gathers them within the embrace of love, and makes them one with the holiness that God is.

Getting rid of the ideas you have about God is not an easy task, since it can precipitate panic. Modifying the associations you have with life, with God, with what you are, is something to be done step by step, since you can only release something when you are ready to do so. Remember that the Holy Spirit accepts your timing and ways. There is no rush, no hurry of any kind.

III. God Is Everything

My beloveds, you know that the human mind has a strong inclination toward the concrete, which makes it difficult for it to understand and accept the pure abstraction of self. Given this, God created the divine elements that would fit perfectly to the reality that you live, or think you live, on the physical plane.

The Holy Spirit is that part of the pure potentiality and abstraction of God which keeps the boundlessness of the divine alive within you. We could say that the Holy Spirit is the infinity of God extended to you.

Spirit has no attributes, nor can it be defined by concrete words. Therefore the Spirit of God that lives in you, which is what Holy Spirit means, likewise encompasses the love beyond attributes that God is. The Holy Spirit is the infinite aspect of God's love.

God the Father is the divine authority extended to your mind. It is the law of love within which everything exists. A divine authority, as an idea and as a reality, must exist in you, for a negation of divine authority, or of the laws of creation, would lead you to chaos, and would remove love forever.

You cannot live without an authority. Nobody and nothing can. God-Father is the name we give to the laws of creation, which are without limit. Thus the Father is the inexorability of love and power of truth extended to you. This inexorability prevents you from ever being separated from love.

Christ is the Son of God, the filial aspect of divinity. All creation is ultimately filiation. Christ is God extended to His creation, totally dependent on and one with Him, as with a son who depends on his father. The dimensions of God the Father, God the Spirit and God the Son represent all that God is.

We could say that it is no longer necessary to give any other "form" to God. However, given the association of the masculine with authority and with rationality, it is necessary to lay down the Father God once shown to you, and accept the maternal dimension of divinity. To lay down does not mean to abandon those aspects of God, but to allow the motherly aspect of love to join them.

IV. Marriage of Universal Love

What is asked of you now is to be willing to join a God who is literally the marriage of universal love. This creation that we give birth to today is in perfect harmony with the will of God. Therefore it will create a new reality in your world, just as one day the creation of the God-Father-Love changed forever the history of humankind.

God is a marriage of love because everything, male and female as you consider it, resides in God, as well as in all true creation. Creation is born through this marital unity of universal love, in which love remains fused in indivisible reality. Remember that nothing emerges from separation, because creation can only occur through union.

Creation is the living face of God—not creation arising from mental interpretation but from true divine creation, which, although it surrounds you with beauty on all sides, cannot be seen with the body's eyes. The effects of love are only visible with the eyes of love, that is, the vision of Christ. Consider this truth as we move forward.

Jesus Christ is, as is Immaculate Mary, the human aspect of God—God Himself, God in form, God united to human nature. This divine reality is also necessary, since it is almost impossible for the human mind to think without a body. The limited mind adjusts everything based on form, seeking to shape things in order to understand them in its own way. As you know, the physical universe is a universe of limits; therefore it has to be a "concrete" universe. This is the life of matter.

Material thought imposes limits on the mind that hinders ideas of infinity. Since God is infinite, the limited mind cannot comprehend God. Thus Jesus Christ is God extended in form to a human body.

God the Father, God the Son, God the Holy Spirit, Jesus Christ and Immaculate Mary make up the totality of the created aspects of divinity so that they may be extended to all that you are. In other words, Jesus Christ, always united to Immaculate Mary, is all that God is, gathered in physical nature.

Can you begin to see how much God loves you, you who has never left being united to Him? Can you see how the dominoes begin to fall, how the dots connect? Can you realize that whatever you believe, you cannot separate yourself from God?

Nothing can limit love. Believe me when I tell you that if you were to become a light tomorrow, God Himself will become a light with you and His heart will keep beating to the beat of yours. My brother, accept the fact that you cannot separate yourself from love, because you cannot separate yourself from what you truly are. You cannot separate yourself from life. You cannot separate yourself from God, nor He from you.

2.

The Bosom of God

A message from the Voice of Christ through a Choir of Angels,
in the presence of Archangel Raphael and Archangel Gabriel

I. Prelude

My beloveds, today we manifest ourselves again as a sensitive presence. We thank you for your willingness to hear the voice that the Divine Wisdom of Heaven wishes to give to the world through you. In the name of the love that God is, we thank those who receive this work and welcome them with love and humility.

Those who join this angelic manifestation are those whom the Creator has called from eternity to join the new consciousness of the Second Coming of Christ, the new prophets of the end times.

Nothing happens by chance. God does nothing in vain. You who receive these words are literally part of the one hundred and forty-four thousand announced. Your new garments shine radiant in the whiteness of Mary's virgin purity.

Children called by the Lamb of God, we are reuniting you, calling you in from all the corners where you find yourselves, not only in the physical plane, but in created dimensions. You are living in the final times, the times of the unification of love.

Beloveds of the Lamb! You have a sweet mission to carry out. To fulfill it will be your fullness in time, making you a bridge between Heaven and Earth through which divine grace will flow. We, a Choir of Angels of God, are immensely grateful to you for allowing us to be part of your mission and your reality as prophets of the advent.

We know that we reach the fullness of self by giving ourselves, just as all creation does. To serve each of you is to serve love, which is why collaborating with you is cause for joy. To serve is to unite.

Thank you, souls in love, for including us in your life.

II. One God

True light of lights! What joy to travel together on a path that will transcend polarity, for we recognize the duality that we have projected onto God.

The idea of a God-Father was perfect for the stage when you were not yet ready to accept that you and your Father are one.

Now we leave aside the idea of a God who was almost exclusively of fatherhood, and immerse ourselves in Divine Motherhood—not that one replaces the other, but that they unite in your mind and heart, from which the truth of the One God in you arises.

Since to realize this transcendence we have to start somewhere, we begin by recognizing that in the whole physical universe no relationship is of greater intimacy than that of a mother and a child in the womb. In that relationship one cannot live without the other. They are a unit, as is the relationship of God with the Christ of your self.

You live within God. God contains you, embraces, and imbibes everything you are. The life of God is the womb in which you exist, grow, and develop in peace and blessings. In this way God is the Mother of all living beings.

Once you accept that you are one with life, one with God, and are together a unit just like a child in the womb, you can begin to live in the reality of the bosom of God.

To return to the Divine Mother is to return to God. To return to the womb of the Mother is to return home to the Kingdom of Heaven.

Let us begin the final stretch of the path toward awareness, or restoration, in memory of the oneness in which we are created by God. The path that I invite you to travel now is short, direct, and safe. This path to the maternal bosom of God begins with one of its most visible aspects—Mother Earth.

In Mother Earth you can observe and experience the providential aspect of Divine Motherhood, its beauty and harmony. Observe how, through the Earth that you have been given, the Mother nourishes the child. Experience how life embraces you everywhere.

Just as a suckling child is fed by the mother, so the Divine Mother feeds you with the fruit of the Earth. Through the sun She gives you warmth and joy. The waters quench your thirst. Trees give you shade when you need it, or for you simply to enjoy a peaceful rest. The grass offers softness to your feet; the wind caresses your body. The beauty of the Mother is manifested in the flight of birds and the perfume of flowers that brighten your life with their fragrances and colors.

III. The Land of God

To honor the Earth and its creatures is to honor the Divine Mother, is to love God. If you observe with love and truth everything that surrounds you in the physical universe, you can see how God-Mother has foreseen and provided everything necessary for the life of Her children. Could you really believe that your Divine Mother would forsake you when you self-excluded from paradise?

Remember that your pain is the pain of God, and that your decision to separate from love tears at the heart of Christ. We want to remind you that everything you do has an effect on God. Your fate and that of your Creator are at least as closely bound together as the fate of a mother and the child in her womb.

When you decided to forsake the arms of love, your Heavenly Mother had no choice but to let you go. She did what every loving mother does in those circumstances: made sure that you had everything you needed to be safe and sound, and that you could return without complication when you wished.

Remember, you cannot travel anywhere that is not part of God, because God is the whole of everything. Thus the Mother not only provided the necessary measures, but also accompanied you on your trip, and made an appearance in that land, although she was forced to respect the prudent distance that your decision demanded.

Did you think the One who called you into existence and gave you life would leave you to your fate? You can demand that the Creator of life respect your decisions, but you cannot demand that She abandon you. Love never abandons.

Brothers and sisters, even the air you breathe is a gift from Divine Mother, because She is in it.

Bless the creations given on Earth; in doing so you bless the Mother of the living, you bless God.

All beings on Earth are your sisters and brothers. Do they not share the same home and come from the same land that feeds all? Everything that is an aspect of creation is part of you, and this is also true of the body.

It should tell you something that what all living beings are made of is in common with what you are made of.

My daughters and sons, you are not so different from the animals, plants, and atmosphere. Nor are the angels of God, nor God Himself. You are one with everything and they with you. This truth is also reflected in physical nature. Everyone needs each another.

You cannot live without feeding yourself, and you cannot be fed but from that part of the Earth whose function is to feed you. Those aspects of physical creation that provide your healthy eating are like the blood that flows from the mother to the child in her womb. This flow from the Earth to Her children, both animate and inanimate, would not exist without the flow of God's love.

Can you see the analogy between the flow of life from God to you in spirit and truth, and the continuous flow of life on Earth, which nourishes your existence while you remain in time?

Who gives you the air you breathe? Who makes the sun rise every morning? What is it that makes crickets sing? What is that that gives life and movement to everything that is alive? Who gives atoms the intelligence to assemble in certain ways, forming countless beings, everything in perfect order? The Mother of the living—God.

Brothers and sisters all over the world! Love your planet and everything that is part of Her as the home of God, for wherever you dwell, your Creator also lives. God loves all things. Do the same.

Love the temporal life for what it is: a loving and perfect means that has been given to you to reach the eternal. And love eternal life for what it is: your destiny, your inheritance, and the reality of your self.

3.

The Dream of God

A message from Archangel Raphael

I. Prelude

Lights that illuminate life! I am your beloved servant, Archangel Raphael, friend of your soul. I love you with all the love of God. Your life is important to me. You are valuable. I always think of you. You are my dream and my joy, because I share with God your dreams of greatness and fulfillment for all your children.

Yes, dearest brothers and sisters of mine, I share the same will with the Creator: that you accept the eternal gift of perfect happiness, so that we can always live in our mutual company.

He who has brought into existence everything that is has a dream for all His filiation, His kindred. That dream of the fullness of love will replace the dream of forgetfulness. We are walking toward full realization of that dream of God—actually the restoration of the memory of your full realization, for you are the one created.

In the divine dream, the plan of the Creator, all filiation returns to the unity from which it arose, and remains in the beauty, harmony, and holiness that come from Him.

In Her dream, Divine Mother disposes endless bliss, eternal revelry, and the end of tears. Her dream is to live with Her children in a Kingdom of Love created by Her in Her likeness, to be Her joy and Her offspring. Hers are dreams of unity and true joy, dreams of eternal love.

I reveal this so you continue to remember that your worth is above all concepts and words. The beauty, holiness, and greatness of who you are is indescribable. By God's design it is revealed for you to begin to face the polarities of the dual mind and transcend them.

You had a dream for you. God had another. Yours was a dream of separation; Hers a dream of eternal union with Her son. Your dream was a nightmare; Hers the endless joy of truth.

Brothers and sisters, God's dream is a certainty for you. Don't deprive yourself of the Grace of knowing Her increasingly. In the depth of your mind know what the Heart of God is for you and remain united to love, from where you create a reality in harmony with holiness.

Be silent. Judge nothing. Simply join with love in stillness and wait for the revelation of God's plan. Because God is infinite and inexhaustible, revelation of Her can happen in every moment and forever. You can always know more of God, because God never ends.

Since this work is directed at the healing of memory, the memory of God dawns in you with all its luminescence and beauty. We repeat this for the benefit of the forgetful mind.

II. From the Dream of Love to Its Reality

To fully awaken from the dream of forgetfulness it is first necessary to become aware of the dream that God dreamed for Her child, the dream that led to your creation. Then you can move towards the full realization of that dream in your life here, now, and forever. There is no separation between what you are now and what you are always in truth.

God's dream, Her perfect plan, must encompass your existence as it is now and also be able to continue throughout eternity without disruption. If this were not so, there would be a gap between the life of time and the life of eternity. This is not the case, because there is no such thing as Heaven there and Earth here.

Sons and daughters of Divine Love, embrace this message now in the silence of your heart: The life of your self is God's dream come true.

As you begin to allow the memory of this truth to dawn, answer this question: Do you despise or attack any brother or sister who accompanies you for a short time on the journey you make towards your heart?

To attack anything in creation is never necessary. It never was. All those absurd ideas that you harbored about the superiority or inferiority of beings, both physical and spiritual, was an inevitable response of the ego, that totally fearful state of consciousness. It was unnecessary and not part of God's dream. God's plan for you does not include fear because it does not include loss of any kind.

God dreams that you have a serene and peaceful life, finally living forever in the truth that you have already accepted, which is that everything, including you, shares forever the sanctity and benevolence of the same Source of eternal life.

Think of your sisters and brothers—and this includes not only humans, but all that exist—as those who for love have decided to travel with you on the fascinating journey of life. Be grateful to those who are your companions.

You are also a companion of those who also decided to come to the world of time with the holy purpose of helping others return to the Father's house. They could not return to love without you for the simple reason that if you did not exist, they would not exist either.

Your companions and every aspect of creation not only accompany you but give you existence. If only you were to exist, you could not know of your own existence because it is in your sisters and brothers, and in every situation of life in time, where you can—and must—know yourself.

If only you were to exist, you could not know yourself, you would be unconscious—a state of unconsciousness similar to that of a baby inside the mother's womb.

Just as the child comes out of the womb in order to know life and live it, similarly you have emerged from the womb of holiness so that the life of God may be manifest.

We have already spoken of the immense debt of gratitude we have for the saints who accompany us in life. This includes circumstances and situations in addition to both the living and inanimate beings of the entire universe. A debt of gratitude should not be a weight on your shoulders, nor create guilt, but is something you must assume to transform the diminished sense of gratitude that you often show towards life.

Every breeze is a kiss from your Divine Mother. Every ray of sun caresses your skin. Every murmur of fresh water is music for the child of God. Each part of creation is an aspect of the face of love.

III. The Network of Life

The return to the love that God is begins when you deliberately decide to love the Earth and everything that is part of it—that is, when you decide to love what you are and all your circumstances. Do you think that animals, plants, and the elements do not feel your love? They do. Everything around you is susceptible to the divine energy of love, as well as the energy of fear.

I assure you that every act of heartbreak contaminates the world, more than the thousands of factories producing toxicity. In actuality, many of these systems are a result of heartbreak and the underlying cause of pollution.

If you want change, it does not make sense to focus on surface manifestations. Behind the toxifying of Earth lies fear, and behind fear is love denied.

Would you fill the Earth with toxins if you knew that they prevented the life of beings invisible to your eyes, if you knew that they were your children? Have not you been told that Divine Motherhood is something that you share with She who gave you existence?

You are one with the Mother of life. You are one with the Source of creation. Therefore everything that exists comes from you in union with God. It cannot be otherwise, even though you may find it hard to believe.

Each leaf of each tree, as well as the wind, the waters, the fire, the fireflies of the night, the moon and the cheetahs are also your creations and your children.

Creation is not alien to you, not only in terms of its essence, but also in terms of your will, for God did not create everything that exists without your loving consent. Everything happens within that union. The creative act is always universal. In the One Mind that God is, and in which you exist, everything is in unison and in union.

It was you who, with God, created everything along with every aspect of creation. Everything was brought into existence through the cry of love that breathed out from the heart of the Mother of life.

That one aspect of life has one type of consciousness, and another aspect has another type, does not make either superior or inferior.

That the head can think with the brain does not mean that the heart is less important, nor the foot, nor the hand. Everything is part of a whole. Life has no disconnected parts.

Do you think that when you sing a love song to a rose from the depth of your loving heart, she does not receive those vibrations? Nothing you think or do is neutral. Nothing at all.

An intricate web of infinite interconnections, or relationships, holds all creation in perfect union whether or not you are aware of this network. Even though you know not the laws that govern the entirety of creation, they are nothing to be feared.

Not a single atom or element of physical matter is disconnected from all the rest. This is not a novelty for many of you, yet it may be a novelty that behind this infinite network of infinite interrelationships is love, giving it shape and life in every moment.

This web of life is the expression of God's love. Thus we say that physical creation is the body of Christ. It is God knowing Herself through expression in form. It is the Son of God come from the womb of the Mother. It is love giving birth to love.

4.

Love without Conditions

*A message from the Voice of Christ through a Choir of Angels,
in the presence of Archangel Raphael and Archangel Gabriel*

I. Love and Totality

If you love some more than others, or if you love certain aspects of creation in a different way than you love others, then you do not understand what love is.

God loves all things, because everything has come from Her. There is nothing God does not love. While you have been taught that God cannot love sin, and that is true, you must understand that it is not because She does not love you, but because She knows it is not real. Christ knows no shadow of sin. This not-knowing of the Christ of God is the perfect guarantee of your return to unity.

Those united to the living Christ in them no longer see sin because they know that sin does not really exist. Perhaps they continue to experience the instinctive repulsion that produces everything out of harmony with the beauty and sanctity of love, but that is not due to a lack of love, but because love can only love what is similar to itself. To love is to unite.

Once you decide to return to unity with the Christ you are, you live only united to what is holy, beautiful, and perfect. But you also recognize that there are different states of consciousness and that, among those different states, there is a state of amnesia of self. In that state, which you have also shared with your brothers and sisters, you can imagine many things, even some that do not make sense. However, none of that becomes an excuse not to extend love.

You have already learned by revelation that nothing can limit love. You also know Who the love is that extends through you by Itself. You have learned enough to put yourself aside, and locate your place as God's channel.

Now you know what it means to forgive: Forgiveness consists simply in letting go of everything that is not true. That is how, for everything that comes from the state of amnesia—whether in yourself or in your sisters and brothers—let it come and go like the leaf litter that the wind brings and then carries away.

You accept what is, as it is. You accept that the temporal is temporary—born in time and ending in time. You accept that reality without judging it, without getting angry about it, without attacking those who temporarily accompany you on the journey of life within time on the way to the House of Truth. You cling to nothing. You neither dominate nor possess. You then begin to live without fear, without fear of loss, which is the basis of all fear. You only live in love.

II. Love and the Conditional Mind

Love cannot be recognized through conditional thinking. Life conceived from the linear thinking of "if this, then that" is a limited life separate from the life of God.

Not only does love have no limits, it is not separate from you. Thus you must be unlimited. There is no reason for you to be a conditional self, for what you are is unlimited. This is eternally true.

While you have been told countless times that you are not a limited nor an insignificant self, you are now being reminded again that this truth will not make sense to you nor will it create any lasting change in your life if you do not viscerally accept that you are only love.

You are not a human being, nor a certain character, nor a mother or father who takes your children to school, nor a doctor, nor a monk. You are love and nothing but love. You are love!

From the reality of the love that you are, you do what you do without ever ceasing to be love. Once you accept this, then you become love expressing itself as a human being, as a doctor who heals out of love, as a loving father or mother who takes your children to school out of love. Love can be all these things and much more. Is this not the same as saying: Love and do what you want?

Love can take any form. Love can be sun, rain, wind, song. Only love is unlimited. Only the love that God is, is unconditional. This is why, again and again, you are invited to remember who you really are. You cannot access and remain in the consciousness of unity—and therefore in your eternal unconditionality—if you believe yourself to be anything other than love.

Moreover, you cannot remain in the consciousness of Christ if you do not unconditionally accept the fact that everything around you is love expressing itself. Your sisters and brothers are love. The creatures of the Earth are love. The moon and a snowflake, with all their beauty, are love. Everything that is real is love. Nothing unreal truly exists.

To live as the love you are is to live in the goodness of truth. To live differently is to live outside truth and therefore in slavery—

not slavery in truth, but in your perception. We make this clarification so that you remember that believing in what is not true does not make what you believe true. Truth is how the amnesia in which you have been submerged will heal.

Since what you believe has no real effect on the truth, be unconcerned about what you think your life was or will be. Rather, this truth will liberate and take you serenely to inner peace; you will discovering that you have not affected the beauty you created in union with the Mother of life.

Nothing true can be attacked, nor even changed. The truth is eternally true. It cannot change nor be obliterated. Nothing that is not similar to itself can even approach it, because nothing that is not true can be real, for truth is the only reality.

III. Truth and Unity

Truth joins love and love joins truth. Love is the foundation of truth; they are a unit. Neither was created before the other. Nowhere does one exist and the other not. Nor is there a place where one ends and the other begins. Love and truth are the continuum of divine reality.

What is eternal has neither beginning nor end, so no conditions exist in God. Love is unconditional. From this flows the need to release the habit of thinking conditionally. If you love someone for a quality in them, be assured that you are not loving at all. Love cannot be narrowed to a person or condition; it simply knows nothing of limitation.

Can you begin to understand why you are asked to observe how little love is sometimes given to those beings who, although having a form different from yours, are your sisters and brothers, as holy as you? Do you think flowers do not go to Heaven? They do.

Everything returns to the love from which it arises. Nothing in creation is lost. Not a single child of God fails to return to the love that gave them existence. From love they come and to love all return.

Believe me when I say that if you walk in the presence of love, snakes will not bite you, nor anything poisonous sink its teeth into you. As you go along the path of life, like the living Christ that lives in you, your dense body is being cast aside, and the subtle self that you are—which is veiled to many and sometimes even to you—will come forward and you will not be what you were.

I ask you now with all my heart to accept that you have the power to perform miracles, and to bring Heaven to Earth. That power comes from Christ. Christ is the identity created by God with which you truly share all creation. Accept that Christ's abilities are yours as well.

Nothing that belongs to God can be alien to you because you no longer live apart from Christ who lives in you. Prayer is the vehicle of miracles, and you have already seen miracles performed through you. It is one of the capacities of which you must take charge.

Recall that when we spoke of taking the cross and following me you were invited, and given the means by which, not to suffer but to take charge of the divine self you are in truth. Become aware of the power of miracle-working that is yours. When you live in the truth, you but accept the power of Christ in you, a power without conditions.

Why do we speak of the power to perform miracles that resides in you as a Christ when we also speak of unconditional love, and the need above all to love all things and beings on

Earth? We speak thus because you are asked to work the miracle of the union of the divine and human in your present reality.

Jesus demonstrated that his power came from a source not of the world, but of almighty God. You need not demonstrate that again, but you do need to serve humanity by bringing the love of God to the world.

IV. Truth and Miracles

Miracles are a service to humanity. The world needs healing, and this is the service you must bring to it. You know how. Every time you join in prayer with your self, which you can do at every moment, the miraculous power of God's love flows naturally.

You can ask for specific miracles or not. You can ask for none at all. It matters not. The power to perform miracles, whose source is always love, will unfailingly manifest.

Brother, sister, cease putting limits on who you are. Love all things. Open the floodgates of your self so that the ocean of God's infinite love—which resides in your heart and expresses itself in multiple ways—spills into all creation more forcefully than ever.

You are to flood the Earth with the miracles of love. You are to heal the universe through the union of prayer with the living Christ in you, which is the prayer of truth. Abandon limitation! Live as Christ taught.

Show unconditional love so as to be more aware of the love you truly are. Thus your love will call others to love.

When you are asked to accept your power to perform miracles and bring Heaven to Earth, you are being asked to accept unconditionally that you can live in truth, that you can live without fear. In other words, accept that you can be the living Christ here, now, and always.

Accepting the power of God in you is part of taking charge of the new self you are. This acceptance is also an expression of unlimited trust in the love that you are. It is something you must exercise, not in the sense of striving, but in the sense of actively accepting.

Until the arrival of this work you had seen acceptance as something you did not like: that you had to accept what you had not previously. That phase was on the path to the transcendence of acceptance.

While you may argue that you do not necessarily have to accept something you do not like, the truth is that you know that everything that is denied is denied for some reason. Denial is not an involuntary act; it is a mechanism of protection arising from fear. Something true is never denied out of love. Nobody denies what they love. The denial of truth results from a lack of love of truth.

You no longer live in the time of deceit, when life moved to the rhythm of the senseless dance of deceiving and being deceived. We have returned to truth, and therefore move to the rhythm of the desire to love and be loved. It is no longer necessary to continue with denial mechanisms.

Darkness has dissipated, and the fog evaporated. No dangers are in sight. The path is clear. The sky is cloudless. Everything has returned to light. In the past your mind created a mechanism to protect yourself from what you believed to be powerful and harmful. How could you not, were it real? Here is yet another opportunity to be lovingly compassionate to yourself and your sisters and brothers.

Cease to judge and blame yourself for what you once denied, for fear of seeing it face to face. The fears have disappeared, never to return. The clay idol that once so frightened you has disintegrated with the rain of grace that from Heaven constantly falls on you, showering you with the waters of holiness.

Now we live beyond acceptance. The process of accepting what you do not like in order to transcend it is over. Today begins, literally, what active acceptance has brought you as a blessing, together with the holy gifts of forgiveness given and received. We have advanced. We have transcended the limitations.

We accept the holiness we are. We integrate mind and heart with the power of love. We recognize that we are powerful because we live in truth. We accept our divine power unconditionally. We return to love. We recover full confidence. We are free. We are Christ, living life in God.

5.

The Abode of Knowledge

A message from the Voice of Christ through a Choir of Angels, in the presence of Archangel Raphael and Archangel Gabriel

I. The History of Humanity

Beloved brothers and sisters, with gratitude we make an appearance in your life, and in that of humanity, to continue extending the wisdom of love.

With this opportunity, we wish to have you understand in a simple way what life is about. We do not propose to reconfigure your life by way of a new mental scheme. You already know that truth is not accessed through the thinking mind but through revelation, which comes from the union of love and reason in the fullness of self.

We speak of a state of fullness not from the perspective of a passing well-being or an elusive joy, but from uncreated truth. Long ago you realized that something seemed to have gone wrong in creation. You searched for an answer but could not find it. That something is what we will discuss here, so that you definitely restore in your memory the truth that replaces illusion.

The history of humanity can be summarized simply: it is humanity's search for its true identity. It is a drama of conflict and argument, as if it were the script of a play. Without conflict there would be no human history as you know it. It is notorious that despite centuries and millennia, the conflict is not resolved.

Every story should have an end if it has any meaning, that is, if it is going somewhere. But this story does not seem to be going anywhere. New characters enter and exit and relive the same drama again and again, merely with a change of sets and actors. Conflict never seems to end.

Who created this story? Why is it repeating endlessly? What is it all about? It is about knowledge.

As you now know, being and knowing are the same. Self cannot be without knowledge. Similarly, knowledge cannot exist without a self, because it must know an "I" or a "you."

The expression "the self, in search of its own identity" reflects the desperate struggle of self to find or know itself, which is the only real need of self. All other needs that you have felt or perceived have no reason to be. The only thing you need know is yourself. Knowing yourself is the reason for life, an inherent need. If you do not know yourself you perceive yourself as nothing.

II. Know Yourself

You can do many things in the world without knowing yourself. Some of them can even be very noble. However, if you do not know yourself, you will not be full because acting in ignorance of your true self is as alien to what you are as snow in summer.

Beloved brothers and sisters, until you fully know yourself your heart will not rest in peace, nor will anyone else's. This is not a punishment from God for having eaten the forbidden fruit, but a matter of reality. This self is knowledge of oneself. How could it extend itself of its own accord without knowing what it is?

Ignorance of self necessarily inhibits extension, and therefore proper expression. It becomes contractive.

It could be argued that simply expressing yourself in the world, if that be the only inherent need, is the right path. That would be true if the path is the right one, be it in the world or not. But this is not a matter of being in the world or not. It is a matter of where you decide to find yourself. If you look for yourself in love, you will find yourself. Look anywhere else and you will never find yourself.

To access true knowledge of your self and thus end all madness, you must go to knowledge in the right way, which is through love. There is no other way. This simply is. This is why Jesus said, "I am the way, the truth and the life," meaning that Jesus is the way to knowledge—the correct way.

Replace "I am" or the name "Jesus" with the word "Love" and you will understand. "Love is the way, the truth and the life."

Can you begin to see that love is the only path to knowledge? Only love is wisdom because wisdom and love are the same.

III. Find Yourself in Love

The fundamental question is: where will you decide to find yourself? Although you have been told not to search, that you have already found, this needs further explanation. When you reach the point of recognition that it is no longer necessary to search—that you will arrive through revelation—this usually follows the fatigue of having long searched and not found. You have looked, missed, gotten tired, and not found in countless cycles, until finally something inside glimpses the issue. You begin to see that the problem lies in not knowing what it is you seek, much less where it should be. How could you not get tired of a circular quest that never makes sense?

Fortunately you are not alone. You never were and never will be. The source of wisdom has placed the eternal truth in your holy mind from the very moment of your creation.

You have been given the voice that comes from knowledge. She shows you the way and reveals the truth. This is why, in due time, spirit increasingly spurs the soul toward the true question—the meaning of life, the only and final question. Regardless of how you arrive at it, everything has contributed to reaching a point of perfect discernment.

The paradox of the search for knowledge, the search for the meaning of life, is that when you do not know what you are, you have no idea what to look for, and therefore you cannot find; but once you grasp through revelation that you are love and nothing but love, you also realize that love cannot be sought. Love simply is. We will now elucidate this paradox.

The first step is to realize what you are. This means to accept unconditionally, with all your soul, your heart, and your will, that you are love and nothing but love; that is, you are the face of holiness, just as, in truth, everything is.

The second step is to recognize that if you are love, you cannot look for yourself. Once again, love cannot be sought. Accepting this may at first be difficult for those who have spent their whole lives searching without finding, which is everyone.

The difficulty of accepting that love cannot be found lies in your attachment to the search itself, and to a mistaken understanding about the treasure of your self. You have found the hidden treasure. The lost drachma has been found. There is no doubt about this. You have found your true self and with it the meaning of your existence.

What a joy to recognize this! The time of restlessness, the time of living a meaningless life, the time of darkness, is far behind! What a joy to be certain! What joy the soul feels living forever in the light! Now you know for sure the reason for your life.

Yet although you have found your self, you think that you have found it through your own effort. That thought breeds the fear of losing what you have found. You say to yourself, "If I lost you once, how can I be certain never to lose you again?" You have not accepted the fact that what you are was revealed to you, not found by you. You did not create yourself.

This is the great revelation: There is nothing to be found because nothing real can be sought. Only love is real, therefore you cannot find it. God does not hide. Your true identity never disappears or gets lost. We have already said that love cannot be sought. If this is true, and I assure you that it is, then it must also be true that it cannot be found. Love is never absent. Love is neither lost nor found.

Beloved sister! Beloved brother! Purest soul! You did not find love of your efforts; love found you. Christ came to meet you and found you. Out of fear of the power of the Creator, in your singular consciousness, you hid behind the bushes of Eden for fear of what you thought you had done.

You were afraid of your creation and you projected that fear onto your Creator, instead of humbly recognizing that what you created without love was neither beautiful, holy, nor perfect. You forgot to stay still, together with love. Had you done that in the first place there would have been no pain or suffering. You would not have separated. There is no need to separate yourself from love, regardless of what you believe you have done or will do. Love goes wherever you go.

Can you now connect the dots and realize that love never hid or went anywhere? Can you remember vividly that God does not move?

Knowledge resides in love. This means that knowledge is not concerned with singular consciousness, since it has no degrees. There cannot be degrees of knowledge or degrees of love.

Either you know yourself or you do not. Therefore beyond the conscious mind, beyond all that the mind can understand and classify, is where knowledge resides. You know that door very well and where it leads you.

IV. The Portal of Knowledge

Now we allow true knowledge, a portal to light, to activate in the memory.

Oh, daughters and sons of love! Our whole self trembles with awe and veneration at the point we have reached. We are here, standing together, holding hands, clothed in the resplendent garments of resurrection. We have emerged from the waters of sanctity.

We stand in front of the doors of wisdom, the portal of truth. Oh sacred mystery of love! Holy wisdom! You are the source of life and love. You are the delight of angels, due the admiration of men and women who seek the truth and the joy of God.

Everything you do, both as humanity and as individuals, is but a way of seeking to know yourself. Observe the force that impels you to "reach your maximum potential." Humans seek to reach that maximum even when they know not what it is. Nevertheless this impulse is proper, since reaching and sustaining maximum potential is by definition the fullness of self.

Let's connect these points. Knowledge is wisdom. As we have already seen, it only resides in love because it emanates from God Himself and God is love and nothing but love. We have also seen how strongly the self is compelled to know itself. We know that being and knowing are one and the same in truth.

Thus we discover that everything, absolutely everything, of what you call life is an expression of what you are in order to know yourself. How does knowing this contribute to your fulfillment? It helps when you begin to tread a fully conscious path about what your life means. To live consciously every moment of your life is to live in fullness. Unconsciousness is the absence of fullness.

You might argue that you were told that you attain fullness of your self by giving yourself, not that you attained it by knowing yourself as God knows you. That is true, but you have also been told that you cannot give what you have not received or recognized.

If you do not recognize the true self that you are, and do not consciously decide by deliberate will to live in harmony with that God-given self, then what do you have to give? Nothing. You would be like a rich woman with her treasures hidden away in a barn. How would her wealth serve her? How could it add to her fullness? Or would it cause her the slavery of having to protect its hiding place and guarding against anybody finding it, lest they ask her to share it?

V. The Dwelling of the Living

Now we reveal a great trick of the mind which keeps many trapped in a game from which few escape. Listen carefully and lift the veil of illusion.

The reason why humans seeks themselves is not because they want to find truth. If that were the case, it would long since have been found and the story would be over.

Behind the search for self is the thinking mind's hidden desire never to find truth. This is because truth cannot be discovered by effort of any kind, nor by any mechanism of the thinking mind. The mind refuses to accept this.

The part of the mind that thinks it learns by its own effort is the part that causes this madness. Even though you have transcended the mind, there are still remnants of memory of the taste that learning provided.

The idea of reaching the truth for yourself and by yourself, the very idea of achievement by your own means is held secretly. Yet because there cannot be partial knowledge, knowledge must reside in wholeness. Thus there is no other option than to get to know yourself in relation to your sisters and brothers and in relation to everything created, including the Creator. And this is what the thinking mind wishes not to accept.

You have been told to stop searching. This is because if you continue with any active search mechanism through mental efforts, you will continue to wander the world under a cloud of amnesia rather than awake from the dream of Adam.

Beloved sons and daughters, let not the mind deceive you. Truth cannot be sought or achieved. Truth makes an appearance in those minds that have emptied themselves enough to allow truth to dwell there, just as love dwells in receptive hearts.

What joy it is when effort has ceased, when there is no need to tire yourself looking for what from all eternity was closer than your own breath. How benevolent is the creative Mother, who has given Her children air to breathe without effort. What a joy it is to reach this point when we joyfully accept the eternal gratuity of love.

Now we hear the soul in love say to his beloved:

My beloved, source of my self!

One day I hid my face so you would not find me. I was afraid you would see the ugliness I had become. I was ashamed of myself. I did not want your beauty to be contaminated by the opprobrium into which I had been transformed. Your sweet innocent look was for me like a spear stuck in the soul. I could not hold my gaze looking into your eyes.

Oh sweetness of my beloved's face!

Remembering you hurt my heart. The very thought of having you by my side shook my whole self. My life was fought between the longing for love and the desire to forget so as not to suffer your absence any more.

Oh beloved of my soul!

One day I hid my face so you would not find me.

But you went out to find me. You searched for me everywhere. You crossed mountains and deserts, seas and plains. You did not care about your royalty, or my disfigurement, or that which tainted my peace. You looked for me and found me. And because you found me, I will live eternally in the abode of the living.

Because you found me I became one with your beauty. Your beauty became mine. The light of your wisdom flooded my mind, at the same time that your love absorbed my heart, embracing all of me, until I merged with you.

Oh, joy of reunion with my beloved! Grace of my God! Oh unfathomable mystery of love! How beautiful is your face. What a joy it is to dwell with you in the eternal abode of the living.

6.

The Tree of Life

*A message from the Voice of Christ through a Choir of Angels,
in the presence of Archangel Raphael and Archangel Gabriel*

I. Prelude

Beloved holy sons and daughters, created in the light of truth, sustained by the love that creates and recreates everything!

We have come once again, wrapped in the mantle of endless mercy. We are the love of God made real in your life. We are the voice of the Lamb extending to the whole world through your consciousness. We are one with you.

We have come as both multitude and unity to dwell with you in the presence of love. By the will of the Mother of the living, in perfect union with your will, we have been granted the unparalleled Grace of manifesting ourselves to give light to minds, and peace to hearts. Whoever receives our words with love receives blessings and miracles, as always happens when you open your minds and welcome the holy wisdom that flows from the truth.

Beloveds of Heaven! The true life of each of you living beings of all shapes and realms is like a beautiful tree. This is the self: its roots are the truth; its trunk is wisdom; its branches are knowledge; its flowers, holiness; and its fruits, love.

Understand well, sons and daughters of wisdom. Your self is itself the tree of life. That tree was planted in Eden and could not be accessed once knowledge was denied. It is now before you with all its beauty and splendor. Access is now free. The cherubim no longer guard you against you, but against what is not true.

Here in this holy land to which you have come, nothing outside of God can enter. The flames of the burning swords that reach from side to side are no longer a barrier to you. The fruit of eternal life borne by the Tree of Life are available to you. It is guaranteed that you will never return to what is not love, because you have returned to the Kingdom of Holiness and will never leave.

Be silent. Contemplate the majesty of this most holy tree. Immerse yourself in its beauty. Let yourself become drunk with the nectar of your holy flowers. Watch and wait quietly until the fruit of love from this tree emerges. See everything with the vision of Christ.

II. The Great Transformation

The universe as a whole—not only the physical plane, but all dimensions—is in an unprecedented cycle of transformation. The energy of pure love emanating from the sun of all suns, the center of all universes and the source of life, has unleashed a process whereby everything that exists is being transformed.

The vital force of all creation has begun to roll in such a way that it encompasses within itself everything that is not of itself.

At work within the all-encompassing embrace of love is a transmutation of the laws that govern material life, from the elements themselves, molecules, and all forms, to the union of universes with each other. It is happening through the transmutation of the relationships that govern the life of each world, creating a complete transformation of everything that has taken form.

You are well into the era of the beginning of the fullness of love, an era without equal, an era of transformation. Love is transforming everything at a speed unmatched in the consciousness of creatures.

The speed of this transformational force of love is unprecedented. Love has always had the capacity to transform everything into love, because form can be transformed; but what is now happening is that this capacity has dramatically expanded. It is permeating all the layers of existence and all dimensions of creation. Nothing will be excluded from this phenomenon of transformed universal consciousness.

Just as you marvel at the creative power of the One who gave life to All, you will be amazed to witness the transformation that Divine Love is accomplishing—and which shall continue until a new Heaven and a new Earth shine in all Their glory.

The new arises from the transformation of the old. It is important to realize that love not only has the ability to create and recreate, but makes all things new without destroying but by embracing.

Everything linked to love becomes love because of what love is. This transforming, uniting force—the inherent ability to make everything similar to itself—is typical of everything that exists. Fear, too, makes fearsome everything on which its dark mantle rests.

If love can make everything bound to it into love, and fear makes fearsome, one might argue that perhaps God can be touched by fear and be transformed into what is fearsome. However, this could occur only in your fantasy.

Love and fear exist in realities so alien to each other that neither realizes the other. One lives in the reality created by God; the other in an illusion never created by God but which only exists in your mind. God does not know fear and fear does not know love for the simple reason that fear is illusory and does not have consequences in reality.

III. The Emergence of the New

Remember: only love is real. Within the realm of love is only what is akin to love: beauty, sanctity, uncreated perfection, truth, eternal life, and the perfect certainty in which all knowledge is integrated. In other words, in the reign of love only love reigns. Nothing in it is unholy. We say this here so that you remember as often as possible that you are no longer the one you once were.

You are a new self, transformed by the love that God is. Thus there is no need to continue to think of matters of fear. That is the old way of thinking, the old self.

Beginning now you will live in the land of the living, and will eat of the fruit of the tree of life until you are satisfied. This is eternally true for you and for all called by the voice of the Lamb to illuminate the world with a new light, the light of the new consciousness of the Second Advent. You need not look back.

Together we travel this path of truth and life. The path was closed and guarded by cherubs to bar reaching the Tree of Life, but the Resurrection has opened it

Sisters and brothers called to be light of the world! We are calling you from above. Wherever you are, we summon you through these words, which are a song of wisdom and truth. As the new self you are, you have become aware to a greater degree of the union of your souls with their source.

You are certain that you have not created yourselves, something you are happy about. Leave everything in the hands of the One who created us all out of pure Divine Love. Be patient with the process of constant transformation in yourself and in everything.

Listen, sons and daughters of God! You who receive these words, listen to us with love and full attention. No matter which corner of the universe you are in, listen well to this call, for it is the call of Christ, summoning His angels to Earth so that day after day you can enlighten the world more with your love.

Christ calls the redeemed to be witnesses of God's love. You are ready to flood the Earth with the waters of holiness, the purest waters that spring forth unceasingly from each one of your blessed souls.

Sisters and brothers! Can you see how this living water is flooding the universe and giving new life to everything?

Sons and daughters of God, remember that creation is not done and over with, but is in continuous movement. We invite you to observe in silence the movement of love. Let's see how the world is transforming more and more. You need not fear change or transformation, because you know its source—your love, emanated from the Mother of creation, expanding and transforming everything.

IV. Recreation

Let us continue to speak of the transformation underway in the universe and in you, a transformation springing from the consciousness of love.

To understand the magnitude of this universal transformation of which we speak—the fruit of the Tree of Life—recall that nothing can limit God. The realm of form is no exception. This remembrance will gently lead us to a greater degree of understanding of God's plan.

Within the creative design there was always the knowledge that form has the inherent capacity to be transformed, and that love would use that capacity for its holy purpose. In other words, within God's plan was a stage that we could call transformation through love of the physical, and with it, all universes. This transformation is the one in which you are living and you will increasingly clearly witness.

Bodies are literally being transformed by love. Consciousness is being flooded by the awareness of the pure love that God is. The self is expanding more and more as the self of pure love. This expansion of love, which encompasses everything in creation, physical and non-physical, is creating a new Earth. This is possible because the capacity to recreate, heal, and transform is as inherent to love as is its ability to unite.

The current phase of the transformation of consciousness within love—and consequently of matter and the laws that govern the union of all things including all universes—existed in divine thought since before the beginning of time. It is not a novelty except for the speed it has taken on and the amplitude of its transformational energy.

Given the unprecedented speed of the force of love, transformation is certain. No one can understand where this change is heading or from whence it comes, because it arises from the movement of spirit, which is like the wind. Rest securely in the unlimited confidence of love. This is why you are asked to trust and why you are asked to abandon human logic, which from now on will not help you understand.

What you will witness will be so wonderful and different from everything heretofore known, that you will be happily surprised. None of the world's forms of logical thinking can help you understand. This is what is emerging.

The physical universe will not succumb; it will simply be transformed by love. Nothing created by God can be uncreated, and the material universe is no exception. Here you may experience conflict with the idea that the physical world, as you perceive it, was not created by God. Yet you have been told that when the mind wanted to create a world without God, God Himself extended into that world of illusion. Remember that God goes with you wherever you go.

In the physical world, because it is the plane of duality, you experience love and the absence of love. This dichotomy that has to be transcended, or rather transformed. Love transforms everything, even fear. In other words, it eliminates everything not of love, everything of fear. Love dissolves and eliminates everything out of harmony with itself. This is how the new world emerges.

V. The Movement of Love

There are beings in the world, beings who walk the Earth, who are incarnations of this totally loving energy which is capable of this great transformation of the physical universe and of all existing universes.

These incarnations of totally loving energy that transform your reality have not only incarnated into human bodies, but also into animal, vegetable, and inanimate bodies.

The transforming energy that comes from the center of the universe—that is, from love—fulfills a purpose and is available to all beings.

These totally luminous beings have the function of cleaning the world, so to speak. They do it solely with their presence. Many of them do not have a specific function other than the regular life of human beings because it is not necessary that it be so. But they have given their assent, "a little yes," which is all that is needed.

These beings of pure light that walk the Earth—reborn from above, resurged from spirit—do not belong to the world although they are in it. Reborn by the love of God, they are living Christs, united to the incarnated Christ. They are literally the incarnation of Christ on Earth and they live among you.

These totally luminous beings are among the one hundred and forty-four thousand redeemed by the Lamb—a mystical "uncountable" number rather than literal number.

The transforming energy of love has entered the physical plane, and it raises new beings constantly because every being can join.

When we speak of the "chosen ones of the Lamb," we are not talking about a select, special group with greater purity than others, but speak of beings like you who have voluntarily opened themselves to the consciousness of love.

Love manifested through the re-creative energy of reality is everywhere. It embraces you everywhere. The energy of pure love excludes none.

The transforming power of love embraces the whole universe and makes its home wherever it is received, in those who dwell in peace, in those who make the choice for love, and in those who live in the truth they have received by seeking it with a whole heart. It is also available for other kingdoms, such as animal, vegetable, and inanimate, because every living being has a heart. Love is not exclusive to human beings.

Here may arise the question that animals and plants cannot make the choice for love, and cannot seek truth wholeheartedly. However this is not entirely correct, since the laws of nature originally come from the consciousness of love.

Each time you dive deeper into loving awareness, that awareness brings forth loving and healing trees. The same is true of animals.

When love consciousness manifests, it does so in all orders of creation. All of creation self re-transforms into unity by reverting to the primal state.

Sisters and brothers all over the world! We invite you to let yourself be transformed by love. We invite you to join the transforming movement of reality which comes from the sanctity of your true self. We invite you to eat the fruit of the tree of life.

7.

A New World
is Born

*A message from the Voice of Christ through a Choir of Angels,
in the presence of Archangel Raphael and Archangel Gabriel*

I. Prelude

Light that illuminates the world! Love embodied! Here we are again with you, the chosen of God. By uniting with you we become one with all that is holy, beautiful, and perfect. All who make the choice for love are present in this moment of Divine Love.

No one is excluded from our love because we love with perfect love. We are a multitude, and also one. We are the holiness of self manifested in different ways. You are you and we are us, yet in our unity lies the truth of what you are and what everything is. We are one without ceasing to be what each is. We are unity in the diversity of God.

We thank you for your willingness to continue with these words of love and truth. Thank you for answering the call of love. We are traveling a path of light. This is a journey that takes you straight to the Heaven of your holy mind; It restores your memory of the truth of what you are, and the truth of everything that exists and moves.

We want to remind you that you cannot see union with your eyes, but it is recognizable by its effects, just as you cannot see the driving force of the breeze yet you can feel the air caressing your cheeks. You see the effects.

We have come to further enlighten your already luminous mind and thus catalyze all minds to union in truth. We invite you to remember that you are one with everything created, just as is a mother with the child in her womb.

You are one and yet each is what it is. The reality of creation is unity, and yet its unity does not annul the parts that make up the whole. Divine unity is a type of unity that is in harmony with God's individuation plan. This matter of unity is of great importance, which is why we bring it up again.

II. Fear of Union

The fear of union lies in a problem of understanding. From it also comes the fear of relationship. Indeed, individualism or egocentrism could be understood as an attempt to be oneself outside of relationship.

The idea of being oneself in a relationship that unites everyone with everything in an undivided unity is something that frightens those who are so obsessed with being themselves that they build fortresses and barricades so nothing pierces the wall of their weak self. They think they protect themselves from possible attack, which they do because they think they have attacked themselves—and indeed they did, although that should not be a cause for concern.

The true self cannot be attacked because nothing can attack love. You can only think that this is possible, desirable, and something that has actually been done. Remember that the fact that you create something does not mean that what you believe to be true is true.

To stop being would be a calamity, if it were possible. We repeat this, for the pain you experienced from the dissociation of self has been of such magnitude that there are still traces of that suffering in your memory. Do not worry about that, sons and daughters of God. Do not worry about anything.

Through this work any memory that is not of God will vanish. Memory will be reprogrammed to perfect union with all that is true. A new remembrance will replace the memory of separation, which will finally transcend all memories and reside in the reality of eternally-present love, the realm of no time where there is no such thing as the past, present, or future, and in which memory is as unnecessary as the thinking mind.

You cannot remember love. You can only know it. When you meet it, you know that love is what you are. Therefore you need not apply any kind of memory or thought, because what would be the point of devoting oneself to remembering oneself and thinking of oneself? Memory arose as part of the thinking mind in order to configure the reality of time and space, where it fulfills an essential function in the recognition of things. Without memory you could not remember what it is like to walk, talk, eat, or even what your beloved's face looks like.

In cognitive memory you store memories, all of which come from the thinking mind. None come from truth itself because truth is beyond remembrance, which is why you think you do not remember God.

My beloved, we transcend towards the non-remembered, the emptying your memory of all content. Just as you have distanced yourself from your thinking mind, since you have recognized that it is not by means of the intellect that you reach truth but by means of revelation, the same happens with memory.

Memory is linked to imagination. It operates through images intertwined with information that keep it in the memory register. Memories are simply information stored in the form of ideas, images, beliefs, emotions, or sensory feelings. Everything experienced in the past has been part of what the mind sought to configure in order to understand experience in its own way. To do so the mind used the relationship between intellect, imagination, and memory. This relationship forms the personality and one's way of seeing life. Thus when faced with apparently identical situations, everyone forms their own diverse opinions. This relationship is established for each self and is not exclusive to human beings but is true for every living being.

Without memory you would not remember anything, even what you are. You could not function in the world. Thus cognitive memory—that part of the mind that accumulates information from thoughts passing from one mind to the other—is an instrument that serves learning. In order to know how to develop in the world you have stored in memory all that you have learned about the world around you.

Now as you abandon learning and open yourself to revelation, what function will memory serve? Although we have answered this question previously, we now respond from a different perspective, linked to the truth that is always true. The new function of memory is to forget.

You cannot stop learning if you keep using your memory to remember yourself, rather than using it to forget. Forgetting is as selective as remembering. If you keep remembering the past, you cannot expect it to go away and never come back, even though the past is not here.

If you do not forget what one day you were, you will continue to delay on the path of revelation. You will be like a butterfly that, having left the cocoon, has not yet realized that it can fly, nor that it possesses great beauty.

You have been told to forget everything you have lived and to confidently launch into the arms of love. That is true confidence. That is to transcend conviction and faith, to move on to what in truth it means to trust. Remember: trusting and loving are one and the same. True love fully relies on itself because it is perfectly known. In love there are no doubts, there is only peace, and peace is only possible in the perfect certainty of truth.

Maybe you are wondering why we repeat in this session of pure light that which we have already spoken. The reason is always love. We cannot allow the forgetful aspect of the mind to be harmful to you.

The mind is accustomed to forgetting whatever does not serve its purpose of survival. That purpose does not serve you now.

Brother, sister, please be aware that you are beginning to forget everything that is not true, everything you have learned. Revelation is beginning to break out in your mind like an aurora on the horizon at dawn. Bit by bit the light is shining more and more. The truth is shining in your holy mind.

In this stage of forgetting everything that does not come from Divine Truth, you may experience, and often will, periods of forgetting—from seconds to minutes of the mind "going blank." Do not be scared when that happens. It is a symptom that your memory is being emptied of content that does not serve the purpose of holiness.

Such forgetfulnesses are the unequivocal sign that the brain, and with it the body, is being transformed by the new mentality in which you live. This, together with possible physical ailments you may experience, is part of the transformation of which we speak. The sooner you release the known, the more quickly this stage, which is always temporary, will pass.

The new being that you are encompasses all aspects of your identity, including your memory, imagination, and physical body. Similarly, your emotional registers and thought patterns are transformed by the force of love that you have accepted. While you are yet in the chrysalis you can have no idea of the magnitude of the transformation being experienced.

The caterpillar has become a butterfly. The metamorphosis of consciousness has occurred. The spirit begins to fly without limitation. And you feel uncomfortable in the new being that you are. You do not know where to direct your flight. Your being observes, is silent, waiting. Little by little it begins to take flight. It rises above all thought and all emotion. Little by little it begins to feel comfortable in the heights. You still fear the fall, but very soon even that fear disappears, for your wings will become more robust than those of an eagle.

III. Prudence and Truth

Soul, friend of the truth! The fear of falling is but a fear of backsliding, a fear of being what you once were and did not like. Beloved daughter, beloved son, know that this is not fear but prudence. In this blessed way of life you have acquired a greater degree of prudence. Virtue is necessary to live in truth and love. Prudence is a virtue par excellence of the angels and of all those who live in the presence of love.

Prudence makes you more reflective now, unwilling to rush where no angel of God would dare go. Prudence makes you patient; and from that patience arises the wisdom of love, which trusts in God fully whether to act or not, to fly or not, to sing or not, to laugh or not. In short, now you can begin to be truly free. We say "now," for this was not previously possible. Without due prudence and holy patience, flying would have been crazy. Enough tears have already been shed because of the imprudence of those who walk the world.

Soul in love, what you are being told with crystal clarity is that you are ready to fly next to the Heart of God. Do not be afraid of the height. You will not burn as you approach the sun, nor will you be pulverized in the presence of the Almighty. No, on your flight through the highest heights of holiness you will feel at ease with yourself and with everything created. Recall that birds are happy flying overhead and slow when walking on the ground.

Rejoice, sons and daughters of God, to recognize that a new being has emerged from the chrysalis of love, a being whose beauty could not be described by human words. The changes you have experienced, and those you will continue to experience, are part of this transformation of your reality.

Remember that as it is inside, so is it outside. The transformation of your being can be seen by its effects. Cannot you see it now? Is it not obvious that you have changed a lot, even though certain areas still remain where change is necessary but seems to come more slowly?

The changes you experience are all benevolent, whether you understand them or not. The child who lives inside the mother's womb changes greatly before being born. Likewise it is happening with you as an individual and with creation as a whole. You are inside the womb of God, being born to eternal life.

It is understandable that at the beginning you might feel a little weird with so much change, and especially with your letting go of the desire to understand with the thinking mind. What you are cannot be put into words; that is why the mind sometimes experiences conflict. Sometimes this conflict can be very acute.

The impatience that you see around you—and sometimes within you—is a sign of what we are saying. It is the result of a world changing by leaps and bounds at all levels and parts, and a humanity that keeps thinking with the thought patterns of the old and does not know where that change is headed. We will address later this matter of not knowing.

Now it is simply enough to say that the multiple transformations you are experiencing are not the result of disorganized chaos but the birth of a new world, whose foundation is unity.

8.

My Beloved Christ

A song that springs from the pure heart of Archangel Raphael

I. Archangelic Love

B lessed souls! Daughters and sons! Once again we are present in a perfect union of Heaven and Earth. In these dialogues of love and truth is gathered everything created. Herein lies the unity of the totality.

We can never tell you too often how much we love you, and through Grace this manifestation is for all. The blessings that emanate from the heart of our beloved Christ to us, and from us to you as a light that envelops us all, is an incessant coming and going that spills over into everything created, just as the wind envelops everything it touches.

Oh daughter or son of light, blessed soul of our Creator! Just as you have opened your heart, stripped naked and unadorned in its beauty, bared in direct relationship with God, in the same way I share with you the beating of my Archangelic heart, a heart created by the Father of Beauty and Holiness just like yours. My heart is one with you and with everyone, for we are one heart. We are united.

I assure all of you who receive these words of the uniqueness of this manifestation. Never before has there been someone who can write of the eternal love that the heart of the Angels feels for

Christ and also for children, the saint beings who with so much love have redeemed and resurrected.

Beloved of eternity, hear my heart. Come to Him. Gather the treasures that your eternal Mother has deposited, for they are as much yours as mine, because everything I have comes from the Mother and belongs to Her.

I speak of the Grace of God and the love of the Creator of the holy, the beautiful, and the perfect. I will speak of your being. You are the delight of my heart. You are the joy of the angels and the joy of Christ who constitutes the essence of our Archangelic love and all love. To Him we pay you all honor and all glory forever and ever; therefore it is right to honor you too, who are one with Him.

You, beloved pure soul, return to the abode of light through your love of Christ and His love for you, the gift of God for all, the blessing of Heaven sacrosanct, you the perfect abode of Christlove. Know that all creation blesses you. You are pure. You are innocent. You are beautiful. You are mystery. You are divine love.

My son, daughter, we cannot separate the beauty of God from yours, nor from ours, nor can we separate it from divine grace. You yourself are the personification of the grace of love; thus you are graceful, beautiful, holy.

Remember, my beloved, that Grace is like the mantle of the night sky that surrounds creation with the beauty of its stars, with a silver moon giving light and mystery to an Earth blessed by the Creator.

Silence, mystery, infinity! God it is who takes care of Her children in the serene night, wrapping them in Her tender gaze. So sweet is the heart of the Mother of the living! That is how loving is your protection, and how benevolent the universe: beauty, magnanimity, life-extending, an infinite creation of love with no beginning and no end.

Beloved soul of mine, receive my love and extend it throughout the world. Join it. Keep it forever in the silence of your heart, where we will live always united in our beloved Christ. Feel the sweetness of my love. Rest your head on my chest. Rest in the peace of my being. I am your beloved Archangel Raphael. I am a light that illuminates. I am love. I am peace. I am healing.

II. Praise to Creation

Oh greatness of creation! Perennial mystery, silence of God, incomprehensible majesty! Madness of infinite love, gift from the Mother to the Son, inheritor of holiness! Who can imitate you?

Stars twinkling in the skies of the night, laughing waters dancing to the beat of joy, wet earth nourishing the children of creation. Trees hug, flowers beautify, birds fly in an air of immensity, fish swim through rivers and oceans, algae float with the currents of the seas, fireflies illumine with their perfect bodies, felines slink stealthily with scrutinizing eyes.

Birds sing to the rhythm of the sun's arc. Rain cleans all. Fruit of all colors feeds the beloved children of Mother Earth. Harmonies of creation! Perfection of forms and sounds, symphony of creative love! Delirium of a God of pure love.

Oh created majesty! Who can know your laws and parts in their entirety? None. None can penetrate the bowels of your essence. None can explain who has given you life. You are the face of God. You are Her body, Her handiwork. To look at you leads my angelic soul and all souls to the contemplation of the mystery of love. To love yourself is to love God Herself because you are God in Her, Creator-created, inseparable union, undivided reality.

Oh holy creation! Who created you? From whence comes your beauty? From where did you come? Who has begotten you and joined you with everything that exists, worlds of infinite worlds that make up your totality? Unfathomable mystery, immeasurable reality sprung from a heart that loves beauty, diversity, and majesty.

III. A Canticle to the Beloved Christ

Oh, my beloved Christ! Creation belongs to you by divine right. You are the essence of filiation. You are the foundation of everything created. Without you, nothing would exist because everything was done in you and for you.

How much beauty there is in your face! How much holiness in your eyes, how much joy in your perfect heart, how much purity, how much love!

Oh, my beloved! My beloved Christ.

Source of my being and of all being, longing of my heart and fullness of souls, to know you, to contemplate you is paradise, is Heaven. The angels adore you. The Archangels loudly proclaim the greatness of your name. The cherubs with their trumpets intone a hymn of praise and gratitude heard in all corners of the universe. God Herself is ecstatic before your presence.

You are the mystery of the word through whom everything has been given life. You dwell in the Mother for all eternity. Before anything existed you were united in love with the Creator. Within the eternal solitude of the most Holy Trinity you existed, together with the Mother and your Spirit of love, living together, rejoicing in the infinite extension of love.

You are the holy abode of wisdom from which all life flows. You are the creative and re-creative eternity. You are the belly of life.

IV. Gratitude to the Human Soul

Blessed soul of the Mother, extension of the living Christ. Know that all creation meets in you. You are the synthesis of the Mother's love. In you are conjugated all elements, all matter, all sentient spirits. You were created by holiness itself as its extension. When you shine in the light of truth you become a word that gives life to your step.

Can you, soul created by God, realize how sublime you are? So much so that even Christ created in you his holy dwelling? You are that which neither eye saw, nor ear heard. You are the ineffable reality of God made humanity.

Remember, beloveds of God, you who receive and share these words, that the reality of what you are resides in union with all that is true. There is no such thing as parts of creation. All is an undivided unity, without leaving the self and you. God Herself has created the identity of each being with the holy purpose of creating in relationship.

In the relationship that exists between Christ, your Soul, my being and all being, is the truth about God, you, and me.

I stand before you as Archangel Raphael since in this identity you can recognize me and relate to me through your self. However, that does not imply that we are separate beings. Everything that is truly part of my Archangelic being is also part of your spirit. We all share everything that God has given us.

Just as a child has everything of the father and the mother, and yet is not deprived of the freedom to make his or her own choices and thereby create a way of life, in the same way it happens with the children of the Highest One. We are all the firstborn children of the Mother. We are the heirs of the kingdom. In our spirits all divine realities are combined because God is the Father and Mother of all creation.

I bless you, praise and thank you for your existence. So does all creation. This praise is not directed to an ego, nor does it denote superiority, but the movement of a loving heart that lives in God. It is an expression of pure love. It is the simple recognition of Grace that your existence means.

V. The Beauty of Free Will

You who have been given a life, a mind, a heart, and a conscience, have made a deliberate choice. The world moved against your choice countless times, always with the hidden purpose of strengthening your decision and your will to the ways of the Lord.

Your choice is irrevocable. Of this I assure you: your choice is in itself a force that crosses the entire universe with a power emanating from love. It has no equal. You cannot imagine the power of your irrevocable decision to live in love.

Oh holy sons and daughters of wisdom! Words cannot be found to express the wonder and beauty of the gift of free will. Can you imagine God creating freedom? Is it not true that many times, at least, often before reaching this point, that when you thought of creative power you referred to concrete things? That perspective on creation is very limited. Think: Who can create freedom? Who, harmony? Who, the human heart, so capable of nobility and love? Who, the human mind, so great and beautiful that it is a worthy dwelling place of the truth, a chalice of wisdom? Who, your will?

You have been told that you have made the choice for love, an irrevocable choice, because that is how you have arranged it. You have fought hard to achieve this goal. Although no struggle was necessary, you chose the path of struggle. And God did not deny you, nor did She make anything insignificant. Rather, because you had given Her the purpose of reaching truth, She Herself allowed you to reach it by that path, not because of your effort, but because of your undivided free will. Remember that to desire with all your will, that is to say with all your heart, is to create.

You have created your own Heaven in union with the Creator of Heaven and Earth. No one or nothing can obliterate your Kingdom. Your Kingdom is not of this world; your Kingdom exists in the reality of love with which you have united. Did you think that the one who said that a single glass of water given to a little one in My name is enough to multiply the love of the Father, was using a beautiful metaphor that sounds good to the ears but has no meaning? No, my beloved. If a single glass of water given by love opens the doors of Heaven, how much more does a human life consecrated to love?

Your humanity has in it the necessary elements to make the fundamental choice for love. You have made it. The life of each one of our brothers and sisters is sacred because at each step the truth calls to them, inviting them to make the essential choice.

The deafening sounds of the pseudo-voice of illusion may make it difficult to hear the voice of Divine Love in the world, yet She calls everyone incessantly from all corners of the Earth and the created universe. The truth presents itself at the crossroads of each one's life. It is afraid of nothing. Wherever a human soul is, it constantly whispers with a sweet voice, singing melodies of beauty and love to draw to itself the children of light. Or it can make the weight of truth fall heavily in consciences tormented by guilt so that they return to the house of the Mother.

The voice of love can never be silenced in any Kingdom created by the children of God. The most that can be done is to deny it and not listen, but it can never be eradicated from reality.

We are beginning to speak of your Kingdom. Little by little we will share the knowledge of this truth. You have a Kingdom, a Kingdom that you yourself have created. This is not a metaphor, but the creative reality of your existence. You are a creator, something you cannot avoid. You create your reality at every moment. You can only create a reality with love or without love; there is no third option.

As a creator, you have to be able to be conscious of what you have created and consciously join it. Your creations are as similar to you as you are to your Creator, because creator and created are a unit.

9.

The Cloud of Unknowing

A message from the Voice of Christ through a Choir of Angels,
in the presence of Archangel Raphael and Archangel Gabriel

I. Prelude

Light that illuminates the world! Beloved perfect creation! Let nothing disturb your heart. Let everything be as it is, without wishing to change anything. Stay in the silence of our union, where the transforming forces of love reside. Remember that all meaning is found in your direct relationship with God.

Do not look for another way of knowing other than that of your inner relationship with all that you are. Every feeling, emotion, thought, and circumstance of your life make up a unity through which you manifest what you are.

In order to understand the purpose of everything, it is necessary to integrate everything you experience into your consciousness. This is how life itself will give you the answers, since she will be your teacher. You will get to know each other more and more.

There is no point in continuing to pretend that you know what life is about. Allow the evolution of your existence to happen as it does. Life teaches through the experience of living, but if instead of letting it happen, you judge it and try to overlay ideas and thoughts and labels on it, and then you make life a nightmare instead of a teacher. You will never be able to give life a definition that will please the thinking mind. Life is too big to be enclosed in one word, never mind in many. Life is God.

It is true that at first it seems a bit difficult to let life be the way it is, without getting involved in it, because you will have the feeling of lack of commitment and loyalty. That, however, is simply an initial phase. With a little practice you will see that you can take distance from events, and the actions you undertake will arise from the place of inner peace, not from the desire to change things or yourself.

Holy of God! We have come in this opportunity, full of love, to share with you and with all those blessed brothers and sisters who benefit from these words, not to intermingle with the life you see. Just observe, stay quiet, and wait.

II. The Love Given

Y ou need not be wound up in the frantic movement of the world. If you are, it is because you dove into it. What can you expect from throwing yourself into the waves of a rough sea?

Sons and daughters, do not jump out of the boat in which you are being led by the one who knows not only how to navigate in peace, but the destination. Do not dive into the mad world. It is not necessary. Life knows how to fix things. Everything has a time and a place in the space-time dimension. Remember that everything born in time dies in time.

Always keep in mind that the only thing that counts is the love given. This is the reason you are repeatedly asked to be open and willing to receive the love of God. Keep in mind that giving and receiving are one and the same. Likewise be conscious that you cannot give what you do not receive.

Loving God above all else is the essence of perfect love. It is the foundation of life. We invite you to return to this simple truth. You have an active Mother of love and mercy. Do not forget. We repeat this so that the conditioning of the mind does not cause you to forget the basis of truth. This is the truth: You were created by God in Her likeness.

You can call to your Mother any way you prefer, for to God that does not matter. It is not helpful to entangle yourself in thinking about how your Mother is, what She looks like, how She thinks, or how She acts.

You know that God is love, and you know love. You know that God is true life and that you are alive. Leaving the evolution of your existence in the hands of life is in harmony with the Creator.

We tell you all this so that you recognize that the cloud of unknowing is the reality of the thinking mind. You cannot understand life through reason. Life unfolds in every moment. You yourself are extending it because of what you are. You interact with it and create life in every moment, in union with everything. Life is eternally being created.

Not knowing is not a sin, but neither is it real. The notion of "knowing" or "not knowing" is alien to truth. In no aspect of life, that is, of creation, can you see something similar to "thinking" or "not thinking," "knowing" or "not knowing."

The idea of reasoning and trying to understand the meaning of things through the intellect should be set aside in order to welcome the wisdom of Heaven. This has already been discussed.

The mind and the heart were not conceived to think and feel. They were created to receive, to receive revelation and love. This is the great difference between true knowledge, which cannot be acquired but is given freely to all equally, and the desire to access wisdom through paths not of God. It is the difference between knowing and perceiving.

III. Access to Wisdom

The decision to seek truth in your own way is the denial of the knowledge of God. This concerns understanding daily life as well. Accepting that you do not know what life is about, and that nobody knows, is a good starting point to access the truth that dwells within.

Everyone has access to wisdom by the mere fact of existing. The wisdom of God is nothing other than Her love. To access it, it is necessary to understand that as God's creation your inherent condition is to be receptive. The condition of receptivity is itself being. Let us explain.

When God created you and everything that exists, She did it knowing that you are a being who receives and, when receiving, gives. She knows that there is no difference between giving and receiving. By giving you your self, God Herself receives your self. By giving yourself completely, by extending yourself, you know yourself. That is why you can be.

What we are saying is that the self can only know itself by giving itself. Here is a simple explanation of the unity inherent in giving and receiving. You give your self, which makes you know yourself and know that you exist—otherwise you would not have awareness of your existence. Thus when you express yourself you are knowing yourself because you are making yourself known.

Life is the sphere in which you pour out what you are. It is the room in which you express or manifest. The different events that seem to arise are but means and ends for that expression. In effect, what you call life is the expression of self. Death, if possible, would be the annulment of expression.

If you do not like life, it is because you do not like the expression of self, which is a judgment. Judging an expression as good or bad implies some lack of understanding. Expressions are what they are. It is important to realize that if you do not love creation, you can hardly love its Creator.

If you say you love the Creator but do not love Her work, you are not living the truth. You cannot separate observed from observer. You cannot separate created from Creator.

IV. The Experience of Not Knowing

Life is experience. What you call life is actually a series of experiences. How you experience the events of life is strictly personal because everything depends on your perception. Thus life seems to be different for everyone, which is why life defies definition.

The cause of experience is perception, and this in turn produces effects. Again, cause and effect are one and the same. The relationship between experience and perception is often overlooked. Beliefs have the power to dictate your actions and with it the circumstances of "your" life, not so much in the external sense but the inner sense—your interpretation or perception of things.

Here we speak of the particular experience of ignorance. Remember, before moving on, that ignorance does not really exist because only love is real, and love is wisdom. Fear is ignorance. There is nothing you can get from fear that helps you understand anything. Instead, fear cancels access to the wisdom you naturally have. Thus it is also fair to say that ignorance is fear.

The fear of not knowing is understandable. It comes from an ancestral source, that not knowing the reality in which you exist would make it impossible for you to continue existing. The ancestral knowledge of this eternal truth has been applied to the making of the world. It is what makes you seek to understand what happens, what surrounds you, the laws that govern the universe, and the meaning of what you are. You use the physical self for this purpose.

The desire to understand, the constant search to find meaning, comes originally from truth. In your heart you know that ignorance does not exist. You know that in ignorance there can be no life. Ignoring what you are or ignoring what is around you would make it impossible to function harmoniously with your environment. You would respond in a chaotic way. That would make the continuity of life impossible.

We have repeated in this session of love some concepts that have already been developed throughout this work in order to intertwine them in a particular way and to continue weaving a new tapestry that literally means a new world.

We can affirm that the old world was built on the basis of ignorance, the new one on the foundation of the wisdom of love. Would not two worlds arising from such opposite sources be completely different from each other?

The search for knowledge comes from your certainty of the existence of wisdom. You understand that the intellect, or activity of thinking, cannot be the means of knowing. In other words, knowing is proper to wisdom. Since you do not know the meaning of wisdom, you used it in a way contrary to the nature of what it is.

The faculty of understanding was not given to you to create a world of effortful thinking or to "have to" access knowledge. Knowledge is given.

The cloud of unknowing in which the old world was submerged is unreal. The certainty of wisdom can come only from the truth that is always true. The point now is to recognize where wisdom resides, where to find its source, and how to live from it, so that you can continue to build a safe and happy world, a world based on certainty. This is how to create a new world.

10.

Wisdom: The Gift of Love

A message from the Voice of Christ through a Choir of Angels, in the presence of Archangel Raphael and Archangel Gabriel

I. Prelude

Sons and Daughters of truth! Bliss of God! We are here to continue together on this journey of the soul that leads to eternal truth. We make an appearance in your life for the sake of the holiness that you truly are. We are the unity of love. We live in a light that never goes out. We dwell where the soul rejoices with the sweetness of love. We live in the holy mountain of your holy mind. We are part of God's perfect creation, just as are you.

We want to express our gratitude to you, once again, for your holy willingness to receive the Grace of the healing of memory, and to leave your mind and heart empty of everything so they may be filled with wisdom.

Come, sons and daughters of light, come sing with us and with all creation a new hymn of praise to the Father of lights. Stay in the eternal Abode of Heaven where love and truth reside, united in inseparable union.

Sing, laugh, dance with us! We are the living expression of the joy of God, as is your self and all self. Begin to live only in light where there is no shadow of ignorance. Begin to live only in love where there is no fear.

Here, in the land of the living, only truth shines in all its glory. Only love exists. Harmony cannot be modified, nor wisdom disdained. Here we live in a truth that recognizes that holiness, like God, has no opposite.

Beings of the highest, if only you could realize how high we have risen, you would begin to leave all duality behind forever, because you would realize that it does not exist any more. You no longer live in illusion. You live in the land of the living now, where the sun and life are one, where there is no night. Your self lives where there is only the joy of creation, extending eternally.

II. Awake

Beloved soul in love, beloved daughters and sons, you have already awakened to eternal life. Let us continue to enjoy this new existence in which you are as you have always been in truth, even though there was a time when you acted as if you couldn't be. Awake you are, dancing the dance of life, singing the melodies of eternity.

Light that will never wane! Within you is a place much higher than the stars and sun, more distant from the noises of the world than east from west.

That place where we dwell with you and with all that is holy is not properly a place, but is literally what you call your heart, your self. It is where wisdom resides, whose source is the Sacred Heart of Christ. Your self is the life-giving force of your whole existence, with its origin in the center of the universe, which is the heart of everything created. Your self emerges from the core of spirit that gives life to everything and creates the immaterial, and then manifests itself in infinite ways. Your self is to God as beautiful tongues of fire are to the center of a bonfire.

Brother, sister, you who live in the truth, you cannot create a safe world that is not based on certainty. We invite you to leave behind everything you doubt or might eventually doubt, for things about which there is no possibility of doubt. Only the wisdom of your heart can provide the certainty necessary to build an existence based on peace. The mind cannot. Further explanation is unnecessary because you have proven it over and over on an exhausting path that is already left far behind.

Centuries of spiritual teachings have taught that what you do not obtain with effort lacks value or that what you obtain with effort is worth the cost. This belief, so rooted in the old world, is a stone that prevented you from moving forward, a stone to which the soul was chained, preventing it from taking flight.

The idea of the value of sacrifice has been left behind except in one aspect, also to be released forever, which we will discuss in this session. To link sacrifice, or effort, to knowledge is an impossible relationship. Nothing achieved with effort can resemble wisdom, since wisdom is the sweetness of love and there is no sweetness in sacrifice. Likewise, you must recognize and often remember that wisdom, like love, cannot be put into words.

Wisdom is the "computer of love." It is that which makes love believable. In effect, wisdom is the law of love. This perfect association between wisdom and the law of Heaven is usually overlooked.

When you observe physical nature you can admire the order it reflects and how its laws are inexorably fulfilled. Nothing in creation is beyond the wisdom of life. Wisdom exists in the nucleus of an atom, in the union of the elements, in the cells, in the relationship between the forces that keep harmony within the vast cosmos. It is wisdom that directs how everything is done.

Wisdom gives creation its framework. She places limits on the unlimited and sustains time within the eternal. She allows everything that the will is capable of without opposing God. Nothing that can be thought or devised can be alien to wisdom, because she is the source of knowledge and consequently of the work of God. For this reason wisdom is the source of the light that illuminates every man.

Is it not true, friend of the eternal truth, that life knows how to manage and keep going despite everything? Bodies may pass, planets may cease to exist, and yet life continues inexorably to express. It will always find how to manifest and continue to create and to extend more life. When you cut a tree or pull a flower, do you think they have ceased to exist?

When God created everything, She knew that Her wisdom would be inherent in creation. The Creator never places limits on wisdom, because to do so would cause life to cease to exist, and with it Herself. God is life and the giver of existence.

III. Wisdom of God

Recognize vividly that wisdom has nothing to do with concepts or with what can be put into words. Thus you cannot but accept the fact that the apparent knowledge of the world, acquired through the intellect, is an imitation of the true wisdom of Heaven.

As extreme as it may sound, my beloveds, you must understand that what you call the "wisdom of the world" is a mechanism of separation. It is an absurd, unnecessary attempt to want to know without the intervention of God. It is the most eloquent expression of a humanity that would no longer need God. Brother, sister, if there is one way in which you have striven most to demonstrate separation and most sought to differentiate yourself from everything, it is with the intellectual. Does not that reveal something? What do you seek when you want to know something? You seek specific knowledge.

Specificity belongs to the thinking mind because it is limited. When you seek knowledge through thinking and reasoning, you are declaring that you can sever truth. That is the belief behind the specifism of knowledge.

The notion that reality can be divided is an idea born of a divided mind, like any idea of separation. It has been elaborated upon for millennia, leading to the current state of affairs in which it is believed that many separate minds, full of specific knowledge, can come together to create a greater knowledge— as if truth is a puzzle and each mind a piece. Or as if knowledge was quantitative. If this were true, you would not be one with the whole. You would not be one with love.

Humanity redeemed by the Lamb has come very far in the way of love and truth. And yet they still engage in affairs of knowledge. Learn to distinguish between the limited knowledge of the thinking mind and the wisdom that comes from Heaven. Its quality is a key to discernment. Wisdom is sweeter than honey, it has irrevocable certainty, it unites, it does not change, it creates life, it is soft as a summer breeze, it is always faithful, it is tender like the eyes of a nursing child, and it lives always in the truth.

Beloved children from all corners of the world, we invite you to release your attachment to intelligentsia in all its forms so that you can finish freeing your minds and freeing your path. When you do so, wisdom will dictate everything that should be revealed to you because of what you are.

Wisdom will inform you about everything in due time. I assure you that wisdom can heal bodies and souls, transform the Earth, create new worlds, raise the dead and make the blind see, all in the blink of an eye. Didn't She create the entire universe by means of a simple "Let it be done"? Do you think wisdom can be limited?

IV. True Knowledge

Sisters and brothers, wisdom lies in love because they are one and the same. Outside of love nothing exists, not even wisdom.

When separation was conceived and we sought to create a world based on the opposite of love, that is, fear, we sought to create the impossible because wisdom cannot accompany nonsense. Nevertheless, the need to know could not be completely denied. That is why intellectuality was made—a way of knowing quite peculiar and of course, contrary to love, the source of true knowledge. The science of good and evil sought to replace the wisdom of love. The rest of the story is known and needs no repetition.

Lights that illuminate the world, the time has come to accept that the only way to be wise is to live in the presence of love.

The problem you have with knowledge, that is, with wisdom, is the same as you have with love: your definition. You try to define love and, with it, knowledge. You actually do so with everything that crosses your mind. Truly, truly I tell you that it is not you who does so. The one that seeks to define everything is what we call the "thinking mind." It has been active for so many centuries that it moves with a kind of inertial force. Do not worry about it. That force is less and less powerful because it is not being fed.

Now your mind and your heart walk together, holding hands. They will never separate again because both have found what they were looking for—completeness. The mind found in the heart a refuge so longed for; the heart found grace in the mind, since the mind is the only means by which the heart can express itself and thus know itself.

Remember, the mind is the active means by which the spirit creates and extends. Life is thought. The mind is the throne of truth. The heart is the throne of love and the foundation of reason. Love without reason is madness; intelligence without love is cruelty. Remember also that the heart is your self, where everything that the mind expresses arises.

Just as you have been taught that knowledge can be acquired through effort, you were also told that you must sink your being into a land of darkness, for if a seed is not buried, it does not sprout. This was not about submerging yourself in the shadows of pain and unconsciousness.

We must be very careful with the teachings received. They played a role during the time they were needed. All of them will persist forever if they are linked to the uncreated truth. However, in the new world in which we are living, a world whose foundation is the wisdom of love, they will be re-signified.

When it was said that you should sink your being into a land of darkness, you were told to let your mind and heart sink into the mystery, which is the source of your knowledge and action. You can now stop assigning to mystery the attributes of fear and begin to accept the fact that God, you, and life are mystery. And you live in peace with that truth. You begin to realize that from the depths of mystery springs a vital force that encloses within itself the wisdom of God. And from that comes perfect certainty.

You replace the cloud of unknowing with wisdom not of the world. You happily realize that the space you once thought was ignorance was really mystery, and you do not seek to fill that space with false knowledge.

You let everything be as it is. You begin to become aware of the relationship that exists between your consciousness and the mystery that you are. From that relationship the truth about everything begins to flow into your conscious mind, and doubt disappears.

Certainty reigns in the mind that accepts mystery, and in the heart that loves to listen in silence. Christ himself becomes the source of your knowledge and action. Fear disappears. You dwell in the land of wisdom that shall never pass away. You become one with Her. You merge in the beauty of love, and enjoy the sweetness of the knowledge of Heaven which lives eternally in you and in everything created. You are no longer alone and helpless. You no longer live in the realm of foolishness. You now live securely embraced by the wisdom of love.

11.

Receptivity

A message from the Voice of Christ through a Choir of Angels, in the presence of Archangel Raphael and Archangel Gabriel

I. Prelude

Sons and daughters of the light! Beloveds of pure love!
Here we are, gathered in the presence of the love that you are, happily singing a song of praise and gratitude to God for having created you. When we see you, we see God. When contemplating you, we contemplate holiness. When we love you, we extend the love that God is. By sharing, we are as God created us because we were created to give ourselves. We thank you who receive these words for allowing us to express our fullness of being. We know, because we live in the truth, that our fullness is achieved by giving ourselves, and that giving and receiving are one and the same. Therefore we repeat once again our gratitude to you who receive our giving.

The one who receives love grows greatly because of the widening of love when given and received. The more love received, the more love given. Love always seeks to give itself and at the same time to be accepted, or the giving would be incomplete. The same happens with the self, because they both are one. Giving is a Grace and a reality of every self. Everything that exists seeks to give itself, express itself, manifest itself, to become known in order to know itself.

Your receptivity allows our pure love to spread and for us to live in the fullness of love. At the same time it makes your heart grow larger and receive and give more and more love. The eternal flow of love that creates new love, given and received, is literally the flow of life. Brother, sister, life is obstructed if you do not receive it and give it. The giving of which we speak is not what you have experienced so far; it's unlike the old way you considered as giving.

"Giving to lose" is nonsense in the Kingdom of Heaven—inconceivable. There are no losses, no possibility of diminution of any kind in the Kingdom. A being cannot be either less or more. The reality of the Kingdom is pure, unlimited extension. Extending does not mean being more, but it does mean growth.

We talk about receiving to be able to live in truth. Only those who are willing to receive God, that is, receive love that is true, can consciously extend the Kingdom, because the Kingdom is God, Christ is Heaven. In this session we speak of receiving the wisdom of Heaven, how to find its source and hold in your mind the beauty of its light forever.

The way to live in wisdom is through full acceptance of it. This is achieved by your willingness to abandon ignorance. Observe how on repeated occasions we speak of "abandoning." This is because the focus of this work is to return you to the power of your will, through which you can make decisions in harmony with Divine Truth.

You are God in God—created by God to be like God, literally in God. Your sincere desire to live in the truth will always enjoy divine approval and with it the power of the miracles and the strength of the love of the Creator. All Heaven bows to you every time you abandon what is not true in favor of what is. You were not created for ignorance. You will never feel comfortable in it.

Wisdom is the reality of your being. You are wise because of what you are.

You are not being asked to be a scholar. You are asked to open your mind and heart to receive in every moment, consciously, the wisdom of Heaven and allow it to be the source of your knowledge and activity.

II. Trust in the Heart

Accepting the wisdom of God that resides in you, as in each of your sisters and brothers, is an act of respect for truth. It is also an acknowledgment of your true self, the Christ in you. In order to accept wisdom, which is the same as abandoning ignorance, it is necessary that you respect more and more what your mind elaborates and your heart weaves. The wisdom of the heart united with the wisdom of reason is the force that has given existence to creation.

God knows for what She created you. She made no mistake. You have not been wrong when you have decided to act, or not to act, from the fullness of the heart. You know perfectly well what makes you happy and what does not. You know very well, without a doubt, what things you long for and what you do not. You know what you like and what you do not. In short, you know.

To trust in what you know from your heart is to trust in yourself and in God who expresses Herself through you. Notice how we have now joined the abandonment of ignorance with the acceptance of wisdom and trust. This is because there is a direct relationship between a lack of self confidence and a lack of trust in God, life, and everything. And there is also a relationship between lack of trust and the acceptance of ignorance as a possible state.

Not trusting that your being knows what you really are and that it acts to lead you on the path of eternal light was a consequence of ignorance. That is why we have said that ignorance is fear and fear is ignorance. They are one and the same.

Ignorance is a mechanism to hide love and truth from you. Being ignorant seems to exempt you from responsibility for your life. The ego created ignorance as an expression of what it is, and would like the mind take refuge in it. If you do not know anything, you cannot be responsible for anything and therefore do not deserve punishment. Can you begin to see the relationship between guilt and ignorance?

Recognize that ignorance is guilt. It is an immature mechanism forged by the ego to excuse you from its madness. We also accept that wisdom is the safe dwelling place where we live in the presence of love. Knowing before acting or stopping to act is wise, as is knowing before thinking or expressing an idea or feeling.

We have discovered with happy amazement and serenity where wisdom resides, but how does the habit of being wise develop? This also concerns the healing of memory, since remembering where the sweetness of true knowledge dwells and how to hold its light is what returns you to the state of security you have always sought.

All fear comes ultimately from ignorance of your true self. Remember before moving on that those who did not know what they are did not know what they were doing or what they wanted. They knew nothing, not because the wisdom of Heaven did not live in them, but because guilt had denied access.

Sisters and brothers in Christ, we have arrived at a very high place. We are here united in truth—here, in this moment of holiness in which the flow of truth and love move freely at a rhythm of pure celestial harmony. We are now in the abode of wisdom, that place of your soul in which the knowledge of Heaven shines in all its beauty.

III. Your Wisdom

The seeds of Christ's knowledge were planted in the Eden of your being from the very moment of your creation. Now the time has come when the tree of wisdom begins to bear fruit.

As you know, you first water a seed, fertilize the earth, and wait for the rain and the sun to do the rest in union with life, so that finally the majestic tree emerges. But you still have to wait a while for it to bear fruit. Waiting is part of both the physical and spiritual laws of nature.

There is a time for everything, although this truth is not necessarily subject to physical time. Wisdom is not limited by time although it manifests itself in time. In each stage of life, in each stage of the transformation of humanity, there is wisdom as required by that phase. A child has as much wisdom as an adult. People of old had as much wisdom as those of today. All are possessors of wisdom. Life is wise.

Trusting yourself is what will allow the wisdom of your being to manifest. You have spent much time immersed in a lack of self-confidence, so learning to do this is necessary. But remember, lack of confidence, which plunged you into despair, sadness, and discouragement, has been left behind. You are not what you were yesterday. You are new and being reborn every day. You are the resurrection and the life. Therefore you need not be guided by memories of what no longer exists. You are wise in your way—wisdom, like love, is expressed in each being in a unique way.

You do not have to be guided by how wisdom is expressed in others. You may notice your sister or brother speaks or lives from their wisdom, but that does not mean that you should blindly follow. Doing so may be proper for children who have not yet developed the proper sense of inner guidance. Yet even a newborn child has wisdom. That wisdom of life is what makes her call to her mother when she needs her and also makes her calm down when in the arms of the one who gave her life.

Does it make sense to believe in a God who is pure infinite love and also believe that wisdom is in some and not in others? Would not this be an act of divine injustice? You know that the answer to the first question is "no" and the second is "yes" because the wisdom of God resides in you. You may call it intuition or indefinable certainty, but it is wisdom.

What is it that keeps you reading this work? What is it that makes you, despite everything, as humanity and as an individual, continue to believe that there is something beyond the obvious that the eyes see? Wisdom.

Remember that we have said that Christ is love and that you no longer live, but that Christ lives in you. Remember also that we said that wisdom and love are one and the same as are ignorance and fear. If we connect the dots we arrive at the obvious truth. Christ is wisdom. Christ is love. Christ is Heaven. Christ is the Son of God in whom everything was created and by whom the Mother creates eternally.

To hold the consciousness of the living Christ who lives in you is to live in the presence of love and wisdom. This is true receptivity.

Take in your mind and your heart the words that follow and you will live in the abode of wisdom, which is there where the soul lives, embraced by the sweetness of love.

"I am the living expression of wisdom. In it I was born, I exist and I live. I am love. Holy wisdom is the source of my knowledge and action. I am the light that illuminates. I am Christ."

12.

The Relationship

A message from the Voice of Christ through a Choir of Angels, in the presence of Archangel Raphael and Archangel Gabriel

I. Prelude

Brothers and sisters in Christ, we have come to dwell with you in union with God. We are the eternal truth come true. We are one with you and with everything created. We are the voice of the wisdom of God expressed in human words.

Children of the truth, there are many who ask about the end of the world. You get restless when you think of it. Hundreds and hundreds of centuries of experience in your minds have told you that the end will be painful and destructive. These images were elaborated in your cultures, while your minds had no relationship with the truth of love. The wisdom that lives in true reason would tell you that an eternal Creator of pure love cannot condemn you to a fearful and painful fate.

Beloved of all times! The world will not perish. God's creation cannot be uncreated. The Earth will not disappear. Love Her for what She is, your temporary home while you walk back to the holy abode of eternity.

Something born in time that ceases to exist in time does not perish. It simply re-enters the domains from which it came, to continue to expand in new ways. This happens with everyone and everything you know. Love makes all things new. Love renews the face of the Earth. Life is eternal.

Souls in love with Christ, some beliefs must be urgently abandoned so they no longer cause pain. One of them is the belief in a difference or separation between what you call "mundane" and what you call "spiritual". There is no such division. Everything is spiritual. It is important that you begin constantly to see the continuity of Heaven and Earth, eternity and temporality. To know that nothing real can perish or be separated from the love that gives it existence is to know the truth. In this knowledge resides a whole universe of holy truths.

II. Blessed Unions

The belief that you lose your loved ones when they die reflects an overwhelming investment in the old belief. If it were true, God would be cruel. What sense would it make that She gave you those who you love and who love you, only to be deprived of them?

You mothers who mourn for your deceased children, listen once more to the voice of truth. Your children are more alive than ever, living an eternal life, and they look at you with love. You will meet again. You will talk about many beautiful things. You will live eternally in a holy relationship. Your union of perfect love will be devoid of the desire to possess and of any idea of separation. You will be eternally happy in the company of those who have truly loved you, and whom you love with all your heart.

Daughters and sons who weep, believing that you have lost your beloved parents—you have not lost them at all. There are no losses in the realm of love. They still love you, but in a perfect way. At no other time or state have they been more united to you than when they left their appearance in the world. You will meet again in love.

Beloveds of God, understand that the relationships undertaken in the world are holy because of their purpose. Although many do try to unite from the ego, those are not true relationships. The ego was an attempt to nullify relationship. In such apparent unions there is no love.

We speak of relationships based on love that exist in the world, that even if not expressing with perfect love, are nevertheless a most sacred place by virtue of the human love in them. All love comes from God. There is no such thing as the human and the divine, both are part of the same unit: Human-God, or Homo-Christus Deo.

III. Loneliness

Relationships with your loved ones, whoever they may be, and in whatever way they were formed, have been established by Heaven for love to accompany you in the world of space and time. Without them you could not remember love, and therefore could not remember God. If your loved ones did not exist, you could not know—or rather remember—your being.

Every time you feel lonely, you suffer, whether you recognize it or not. The time has come to review your beliefs about solitude. If you stay in your heart and begin to feel the memory that the feelings bring, you will notice that each time you felt lonely, you had the feeling of disconnection. A feeling that something in you was incomplete. Something was missing. What? Many times in the depths of your mind you answered this question with a "someone" or perhaps a "something." Thus you sought "that" to complete you. Do you recall that mechanism?

If when you began to feel alone and began to suffer, and if before being annihilated by incompletion, you launched into a search for that which would complete you, it would be a sign that you know that something would complete you but something else would not. This is wisdom.

We will not focus on whether you were seeking for completion was something real or unreal, and therefore could not be achieved . Nor are we focusing on the fact that if you search outside of yourself you will never find anything. We are simply bringing to the light of consciousness the engraved memory of having looked for that which cannot be found. By seeing it in the light of Christ, the pattern of thought and emotional response associated with this memory can now be set aside.

By releasing past memories which have nothing to do with truth, you give way to the memory of God. Memory as you have used it has accumulated all kinds of information associated with survival. These mountains of remembrance impede the harmonious life of the body and the soul, both of which yearn to live in the harmony that Christ is.

You are Christ. That is beyond discussion. You are—not because of your efforts or merits, but because of the resurrection, or more precisely, because of your creation to which the resurrection restored the truth that is you. That is the meaning of resurrection.

As the incarnated Christ you must remember that you are love. Being love means being connected with the experience of love. This experiential connection with everything that love is, is achieved in relationships based on love. The holy relationship is the gift of God to Her beloved child. It matters not whether that relationship manifests with your fellow beings, with Heavenly beings, or with any living being or object. Every relationship is the same, because it is union.

Not experiencing yourself is not being. Remember, life is experience. In relationships with your loved ones you remain in the reality of the love that you are. This is the reason why you feel comfortable with a given relationship, and why you do not want to lose your loved ones. In reality you would wish to keep the loved one by your side because in that relationship you experience union with the love that you are, that is, with your being.

Not being in a love relationship is to not be connected with the loving reality of the Christ you are. The feeling of disconnection, which you feel every time you are in a relationship without love, produces fear because it is a disconnection of the being that you are in truth. This is the reason why ego-based relationships are so destructive and painful. With no love in them, you did not exist, nor did your brother in an apparent union which never completed anything.

IV. The Gift of Relationship

Relationships are the means by which you can know the love that you truly are, or deny your reality. God Herself needs a relationship to exist, otherwise She could not know that She exists, having no way of knowing Herself.

You only know yourself in relationship, as we have already said. Therefore, relationships that have been established fulfill the holy purpose of giving you existence and a chance to get out of the confinement of separation. This is the debt you have with your brother or sister, as mentioned previously.

If your loved ones meet in time with you and you with them, so that mutually they continue to remember love, then to think such a holy purpose would cease to exist outside of time is not to understand its origin in love. All love praises God because all love comes from Her. In other words, love is eternal.

What happens in Heaven with your loved ones and with relationships in general? They remain eternally imbued with perfect love. They are preserved with all the beauty of Christ and the benevolence of eternal life. Everything of love remains eternally. What is not of love is eliminated from the eternal where it never existed. This is the Kingdom of Heaven. In the realm of truth, exclusion is unknown because there is neither the desire to separate, nor the illusion of separation, but only unity. When the truth dawns in the mind and heart of the new Christ, to whom each one is called to reflect with his life, relationships fulfill the holy purpose of experiencing love and thereby extending it. There is no reason not to feel love every day of your life, all day, forever.

In God's plan there was never a need to experience anything not of love. The experience of lack of love was not real; what was real was the pain you felt in believing that what you were experiencing was the opposite of love. That pain came from the fact that, if it were true that the lack of love was real, then there would be an opposite of God. If there were something contrary to God, that "something" would be as powerful as She, but with all the hatred of the universe. Would not a universal hatred as powerful as the Creator of all creation be fearsome? If hate were real, all fear would make sense, and all love would not.

V. Life and Feeling

When in harmony with the divine, you were taken by your will to the intermediate reality of time and space—a reality created to give humans and other beings the possibility of choosing to return to love in a definitive way; you did not want to be completely disconnected from love. For this reason, you can still see beauty and joy in physical creation. You can still walk in the company of truth.

The feelings emanating from your heart are what bond you in union with your sisters, brothers, and all of creation, including yourself. Without feelings you would be disconnected. You could not have relationship. You could not have life, for there is a direct connection between life and feeling.

In every feeling is life because life is feeling. If you feel what you experience in your heart and allow those feelings to flow freely, you are allowing the flow of life to move through you.

We have said that life is thought. Now we are saying that life is feeling. Both truths are one. God is thought and feeling, united in the perfect unity of pure truth and love. The thoughts and feelings of God come from your being through you. If truth did not exist, then thoughts would not exist because they are an extension of truth. If love did not exist, feelings would not exist, because they are the extension of love.

While a distinction has been made between the thoughts of the ego, which are not true thoughts, and true thoughts, which come from the mind of Christ, this distinction is not actually proper.

There are no such things as false thoughts, nor false feelings. You are now ready to accept this truth. There are simply thoughts and feelings. All come from the source that gives them existence: God. The difference spoken of between them does not lie in their nature but in the meaning you give them.

Your mind is like a prism through which divine thoughts flow and are either distorted or allowed to follow their path, free of obstacles. Your heart acts in the same way, receiving the energy of pure feeling from the Heart of God. We are one mind, one heart, one being. This truth must be elaborated once more.

Your mind, heart, and being are constantly flooded by the light of God. Yet they always wait for your "I," that is, what makes you have a "you," to choose what to do with what you receive.

Everything is a gift. Life was given to you, including the body. You have been given your mind, heart, and being. You were also given freedom. All that you are has been given to you except one thing: the most personal decision, power for what to do with what you receive.

What you receive from God can be distorted, not by your nature but by the meaning you assign to it. Your mind gives things purpose. Thus it is you who can either let the holy purpose that God gave to everything be reflected in you, or deny it and give it a personal meaning.

The old patterns of thought and emotional response came from using the mind and heart for the purpose of assigning your own meaning to things. If the "I" wishes to be a "separate self" from everything, it will distort the meaning of what God has assigned, and adjust it to the purpose of making separation real—even though this purpose is unattainable. Many people have sought meaningless goals and have tried hard to make them real.

Deciding you can be different from what God has arranged you to be is an attempt to save something for yourself. It is as if you want to claim something of what you are as exclusively yours rather than given freely from love. This is the fundamental error or sin. Accepting the fact that everything you are is a gift

from God and therefore you are holiness personified, is difficult for those who cling to the idea that receiving and giving are
different.

Winning Heaven by self-effort is the motto of the old self—
an unattainable but worthwhile goal for those who only sought
the challenge of achieving on their own what God had given.

Creating your own world, with its own laws, was the option
chosen. Not chosen was to live eternally as someone who receives
everything regardless of what you did or did not do to deserve
it. Can you begin to see the connection that exists between the
idea of merit and separation? You sought to create yourself—not
because you were evil or a miserable sinner, but because you
wanted to establish the idea that it was possible. As in a dream
you sought to create worlds and more worlds. Dreaming is not a
sin, although it can be frightening. And it's not reality.

VI. Relationship Consciousness

God is merciful. One of Her signs of unconditional love
was to extend Herself into the world of separation
so you could never completely forget Her. She did this
through the beauty, joy, and harmony evident all around you,
and through the establishment of relationships.

What we are saying is that from now on you will begin to
remember God more and more clearly in each of your relationships. This goal is attainable because this is the purpose of relationship as God has established it.

You are asked to do the following exercise without applying
effort. When you face a brother or sister, or in the presence of
your pet or any object, become aware of the space that exists in

and around them. Focus your attention on that space. Become aware of everything you feel and think.

Begin to realize that all are within a universal space that is embracing them. That space is Christ, who makes an appearance where two or more beings gather in his name. Begin to feel the relationship itself, not just the parts. Let the relationship begin to interact with you.

With this exercise of broadening consciousness, we seek and become more and more aware of the holy relationship that holds things together. By becoming aware of holy relationship you allow the flow of God—of love—to do what it would in you. You begin to become aware of the divine process. This is an exercise of memory: remembering the relationship that God is, which is to return to love. That is the goal of this work.

13.

Giving Form to Love

A message from the Blessed Mother Mary

I. Prelude

My sons and daughters, I am the Mother of God. I am Mary, the Mother of all and everything. Today I am present in your sense perception to deliver a message of love and truth. I am by your side every day. I am closer to you than your own thoughts. I am in the air that you breathe, in your soul and in all creation. I am the eternal reality of love. I live in your heart, in your mind, and in your body. I live in everything you truly are. It is no longer you who live, but Mary who lives in you.

I am the purity of God humanized. You are certainly living in the times of Mary. Again and again I remind you of this holy truth so that you do not forget the love of the Mother. I will manifest myself more and more every day to my children. It is the word of God.

Today I have been wrapped in the joy of Heaven, in a joy that has no end. I have come surrounded by my eternal angels, the beauty of the archangels, the magnificence of the seraphim, who bring me to your holy presence on their blessed wings.

I am the always Mother Mary. I am what you truly are. I am me and you are you, and yet we are both an undivided unit. All the purity of God resides in you because it resides in me and there is nothing in my being that is not my children. As you already know, I was created to be the mother of creation.

Today I want to take you more deeply into the understanding and acceptance of this sweet truth of God's love. I am the gift of your soul. I am the perfect guarantee of your holiness. None of my children can be, in their nature, different from what I am.

You are the living Christ. You are not only another Jesus on Earth, you are also another Mary. You are the strength of God and the sweetness of Divine Love. Both realities are an inseparable part of your being.

You carry within you the power of God, Her authority to create and transform everything, and at the same time eternally to enjoy the tenderness of a love that has no beginning or end. A sweetness without equal. You are all that I am as a Divine Mother and all that my Divine Son Jesus is as God-Man.

II. Express the Christ in You

I come to tell you something you know, because you feel it in the depths of your heart, something to tell all men and women of all times: Listen carefully for the sweetness of love.

The heart is where the reality of love resides, just as the thinking mind is the repository of uncreated truth. Let both aspects of your being come together in me.

As I have said repeatedly, I am the eternal reality of the sweetness of love that God is. I have demonstrated this in myriad ways. This is the truth about me. Everyone constantly demonstrates the truth of what they believe they are, regardless of what they believe. Nobody and nothing can escape this law—the law of expression. It is the law of faith. This is the strength of faith, and why my divine son Jesus taught that faith moves mountains.

Faith is powerful because it carries within itself the power of the Son of God, and manifests its reality in union with it. If you believe yourself to be what you are not, your life will reflect conflict. If you believe yourself to be what you really are, and you believe with all your heart, your life will be the perfect expression of holiness, the truth that you are. For this reason please reflect calmly on what is said in this blessed session.

You are truly the Christ of God made human when you accept this is all of God's work in you. By living with this thought every day you realize God's plan in you and in all creation. I give you this truth made word by saying, "My son, My daughter, you are the living Christ who lives in you. You are that and nothing else, but also nothing less."

I know the beating of your heart and the deepest thoughts that you have in your holy mind, so I know very well that you cannot believe this due to a problem of self-esteem. It is a matter of understanding.

You are so accustomed to thinking insignificantly about yourself. You drown your heart as if locked in a cell. Go out and glory in your glory. Untie the ties that paralyze your spirit of love.

I ask you with all the love of the most pure Mother, to begin to open your mind and heart to the possibility that you are the Christ of God—that you can express reality, here, now, and forever.

There is no need to wait to express your truth. But remember that truth is so far from everything known in the world that you cannot use what the world teaches, but only your heart, as a frame of reference.

III. Christle Begotten by Mary

I am the source of your heart. I am the Immaculate Heart of Mary. I am the one who has birthed the living Christ in you. I am the one who once begot Christ in the figure of Jesus. Today I engender Christ in the figure of your humanity, your being. I have also engendered it in a countless number of your sisters and brothers who walk the Earth illuminating it with love and truth.

Since the resurrection, my role as mother-begetter of Christ did not cease, because what I am is eternal. As Mother of God, and of creation, I exist from all eternity because I exist in Divine Thought, as do you. We are both eternal because God is eternal. We are both saints because our holiness comes from Her image and likeness. We are God in union.

One of the problems you have accepting yourself as the Christ of God is your self-concept. The very idea of a self concept is alien to divine reality. There cannot be a capacity for self-valuation, for if it existed, it would mean that your being is susceptible to valuation. Remember, what you are is beyond all value because your value is inestimable. You are life in abundance. You are truth and the way of love.

Something that has been difficult to convince you of is to accept your holiness, the sanctity that you are, and the perfect equality that exists between Jesus, Mary and your being. That makes it difficult for you to believe firmly in the perfect equality of everything created. You are Christ. I cannot stop repeating it tirelessly, since it is necessary to go beyond the layers of self-denigration that for centuries have covered the human mind and heart.

The rubble of low self-esteem has already been removed; what remains is only the pattern of thought, the memory, of what you thought you were. This pattern is what we are removing.

Indeed, the fact that you can observe this pattern and visualize that memory is proof that you have already abandoned the way of thinking and feeling that led you to consider yourself small, almost nothing.

This work is an eloquent call to live your life from now on as you are, the Christ of God. Remember that the Second Coming of Christ did not concern only Jesus and not others. The Second Coming of Christ will be expressed in multiple incarnations of Christ in humanity.

IV. The Christs of God

Countless living Christs will populate the Earth. They will be the exponents of a holy race. We say, "They will be," because although they have begun to emerge on Earth with the light of the Lamb of God, they will continue to grow in number. The light of Christ is being incarnated every day in more and more beings.

You still cannot see the flashes that emanate from the living Christs that walk the Earth. They are humble and blessed, begotten by the Mother of love. Many of them are unknown to the world; some are recognized, as they should be.

The living Christs that walk the Earth live everywhere. They are countless, represented by the number one hundred and forty four thousand of which we have already spoken. Some heal bodies and minds; others channel the voice of God for it to be heard in all corners of the Earth; others create holy devotions so that compassion floods the Earth more every day; others sing, dance, or praise.

Some collaborate in countless ways, helping with the work of God, all full of pure love. All are part of the myriad of Christs inhabiting the Earth. They are part of the mystical body of Christ. They are the perfect expression of the Second Advent. They are Mary's children.

The Second Coming of Christ impacts not only the spiritual aspect of creation but also the material aspect of it. The second coming is about totality, including our bodies. The resurrection is about both the body and the spirit. The second coming will create and is creating a new body, a new Earthly Kingdom.

The coming of Christ is already here. It will be seen more every day. This is why we say that these are the times of Mary. These are the times, not only of the tenderness of love and the sweetness of Heaven, but the times of birth.

I was created to beget Christ and that is what I do, not once, but eternally in all souls willing to become nothing in love— that is, to live submerged in the purity of holiness. You who write these words and you who receive them in many ways, you must recognize—because in the Design it was written that you join these words— that I have begotten the living Christ in you.

You know how to live in truth. You know how to live as the living Christ who lives in you. Do not fear anything. Do not be afraid to recognize that you love God, or that your Heavenly Mother speaks to you and accompanies you every day. Do not be afraid to recognize your direct relationship with God. You would not be reading these words but that you will love your Creator with all the strength of your being. You are Christ. You are the holiness brought to Earth, part of the mystical body of Christ and part of the Second Advent. Begin again today to praise God in the way you like most. Begin today to feel the benevolence of God's call. You have responded to the voice of love and your grace shall not be taken from you.

Do not worry how you will express the Christ. You have been created to receive love and give existence to others through making God known. You have been doing so whether you are aware of it or not. What you really are exists without needing your recognition. Every being expresses itself. The Christ in you is no exception. You have extended beyond the boundaries of Earth. You have created love infinitely. Thanks to you, an incalculable number of beings have entered the abode of truth and light. The will of God has been done because it is your will.

Today is a day of joy—the unparalleled joy of God in the time of Mary. Today we continue to grow a little more in the recognition and acceptance of who you are. I not only mothered Jesus but I educated him. This means that not only do I engender Christ in you through the Grace of the Spirit of God, but I accompany you forever in the realization of the Divine will in you, not because you do not know how to do it, but because I love you.

My joy is to dwell in you. Similarly your joy consists in being who you really are, which is no other than the Christ in you. Any definition other than this is contrary to God's will and is not true.

Take time during the day to close your eyes, take silence, and say to yourself: *My beloved Christ, here I am to do your will.*

Above all remember often how much I love you. As the Mother of Christ in you, I am closer to you than your own breath.

I am the Mother of God, the Queen of Hearts. I am the source of love.

V. Express Love

Beloved of God, you are beauty made reality. You are an ineffable gift. That is why it is difficult for you to define who you are. You know you have been called, but you still believe that you do not know how to express what you know. You know for sure that you want to give yourself completely to God. Thus you already know that you have surrendered. You have heard the voice of love.

You have experienced the purity of a love that has no opposite. You know that the sweetness and love that you have experienced does not come from anything or anyone in the world, but from the One who loved you first. To constantly return to that love is to return to and remain in Heaven. But you will not rest in peace until you give shape to love. You will not rest until you decide to express love in human reality.

Sons and daughters of God, you can shape love. You can do it because it is God's will for you to do so. Dedicate your life to love and express God's will in your own way. You are not alone. I stay always by your side. The work of love is collaborative, not only with the cooperation of your sisters and brothers, but with everything in Heaven.

Those who have to unite with you will unite. In truth they are already here. The events necessary in order to give shape to the love that God is will happen. Things will work in favor of this Heavenly mission. Abandon yourself again and again into my arms. Worry not about what should be done in this holy function of shaping the formless spirit.

Giving shape to love is expressing the reality of God. It is the only way to know yourself and to make the Creator known. It is the only function of all that has been created, just as it is in me, as Mother of God and your Mother.

Everything said in this session you know well because you feel the pull of your heart calling you to the free expression of your love of God, of yourself and of everything created. You live submerged in love. Many already see the flash of rays shining from you, extending to Heaven. Yet even you resist a bit in recognizing them. You still resist a bit accepting that you are a blessing for the whole world.

I ask you once again: Do not deny the world the beauty of your light. If you do not make it known, you will not be able to know yourself. It is the Light of Christ that shines in you. It is the light of the union of Mary and the way of Jesus, united in an undivided reality.

Sons and daughters of triune love, get up and travel new paths on Earth and in Heaven, because they are one. Let us continue together giving shape to love. Let us walk together creating the new Heaven and new Earth, arising from the expression of the Christ in you in these holy times of Mary, the times of the Second Advent, times of the fullness of love.

14.

The End of Words

A message from Jesus, identifying himself as "the living Christ who lives in you"

I. Word of Eternal Life

Beloved of my soul, perfect expression of holiness! We have come once again as the countless expressions of God. We are blessed. We are legion. We are the reality of love made word. We are your holy brothers, friends, and your self because we are one with you. We are one mind, one holy self. We are a single eternal reality.

We burn with the desire to unite more and more with you who you are the Heaven of Earth. Your light illumines the world in a way you cannot understand or see. These words work miracles. They create a vortex of consciousness that opens the doors to a reality foreign to the world, and envelops it in the holy innocence of divine truth.

The effects of this work cannot be understood by the limited logical mind that thinks "If this, then that." That part of the mind, that mechanism used by the mind, cannot encompass the unlimited vastness of the miracles that everyone receives from the flow of the energy of these words.

The word is energy, because it is the expression of a thought. There cannot be one without the other; thus these words, with their celestial energy, produce holy effects. The world is decontaminated every moment you spend with your Creator. Remember that one is never more truly being human than when prostrated in adoration before one's Creator.

I said that I would return in the voice of Jesus. I am here. My words bear witness to the truth. They bear witness to what I said two thousand years ago. These words are living; the Word made flesh. They are the perfect embodiment of my voice.

I will not return as a single body, a single personality, as happened two millennia ago. I return through the living word that becomes flesh in many of you through these words that, when embodied, are expressed in human reality. They are for the men and women of all times and places for whom this love letter is written.

This work is one among many. Every day there will be more living expressions of my word in the world. Much will continue to be written until the time when words cease. Everything born in time will cease to exist in time, some things earlier, others later.

There will be a time when words, written or spoken, will not be necessary, a time when you return to the reality of love in which there is a unique language, the soundless language of love, a language without words, a direct expression emanating from the union of minds and hearts, an eternal dialogue that develops in the ecstasy of contemplation. However, as long as there is a need for words, my voice will take that form, whether written, sung, or spoken.

Enjoy the blessed gift that is this work and all that overflows from the heart, because it is inspired.

II. The Source of Beautiful Knowledge

Everyone can access the source of the living word which dwells in your hearts. There is no difference between he who writes these words and those who receive them. These words arise from the one mind, and are expressed in all minds in unison in a way that you would call miraculous.

The strength of this work is founded not in the words themselves but in their source; not in the prose, or its content, but in the power to work miracles and transform minds and hearts that reside in the union between Heaven and Earth.

The sole purpose of this work is to help you become more aware of the unitive relationship between your soul and God. The goal of this call to live in the truth of who you are is to make visible the living Christ who lives in you.

Do not stay solely with these words. They are but means, not ends. Go beyond what your eyes see. Read with an open heart full of love. Receive these words for what they are, a message from Heaven, written for each of you. You do not receive my voice, expressed in this particular way, by chance. You receive because you have asked from the depths of your self, and because from eternity you have been chosen to receive. Yes, you are the chosen ones of God. Everyone who receives this work is chosen to receive it.

We could say that these writings are the certificate of the election that you have made in union with God. Do you not receive a certificate when you finish your studies at schools or universities? In this case you have concluded your learning from the school of life. Is not that body of knowledge much more complex and vast than a body of worldly knowledge?

These writings sprout from the source of beautiful knowledge.

I am telling you clearly: the time has come to begin to walk in new ways on the path of eternal love, Divine Love, a path both new and known at the same time. I speak not of loves that come and go or that seem to be but are not. I speak of the love I feel for you, and you for me. This is a love that envelops your whole self in divinity—Divine Love, true love, perfect love.

Be generous with these words. Share them as you consider appropriate. Freedom is a precious gift from the Creator of freedom and perfect love. Never give up your freedom. Cling to it as you cling to love. Both are like the wings of the spirit; both are needed to fly.

III. The Wind of Spirit

Words are carried by the wind, as they say in the world. And that is true, because every word comes and goes. The words of the world come from nothing and go nowhere. But my word is eternal because it is the wind of my spirit of love that brings them into being and makes them fly to the hearts that must come.

There is a divine flow, a wind that constantly envelops you. This wind generates the movement of the spirit of God, alert constantly in all created universes in a way you cannot and need not understand. This wind carries my word wherever it should go. This is why you cannot hold on to the experience of God. My spirit blows. My word comes and goes much faster than the speed of light, going from heart to heart, embracing souls with the nectar of beautiful love. My word is music for the soul, a song for the heart, a refuge for the mind, sweetness for the self.

This particular call, made with the written word, is a call for you to freely express your love for God.

In the depths of your self there exists a sacred temple, as you well know. That temple is what you are. I have called that temple "the heart" to denote "the center of something."

The heart has been defined as the center of your self, something from which everything else flows, your center, your essence, where what you truly are resides. It is the abode of Christ, where God Herself enjoys eternally as you. You feel that you know that what I say here is true. To make that inner truth an external reality is that to which you are now called.

I ask you to trust totally in your self. Your voice is essential to the work of God. Do not drown Her; do not allow anything to silence Her. Maybe you have spent a long time without expressing yourself and now feel you no longer know how. Maybe you feel blocked. None of that matters, for you have reached the point where the angels of Heaven, Mary, and I will all accompany you forever in the holy purpose of making love visible.

IV. Your Voice Is My Voice

Allow these words to enter your heart. Make them yours. Do not receive them as coming from an external source; they come from a triune heart and are directed to a triune heart. They are from heart to heart. They are the living expression of your voice because they arise from me, and I am the voice of your heart.

I speak not to a crowd, but to you, individually. I am inviting you, encouraging you, to express what you feel in the depth of your heart, and think in the depth of your mind, about the love of God. Express it in words, in song, in dance, with a hug, an act, with art, or with a smile. Express it with prayer or contemplation, with silence or laughter, express it as you like.

In the joy of what you like to do lies your path of expression of love to God in harmony with your self.

Love needs to be expressed. You need to be expressed. You are love. Until you release your heart, you will not feel full. You have already begun this path of expression; let us continue together.

My love, I am making you more aware of your calling.

Answering the call is essential for the peace of your soul. You have reached a point of no return. You have advanced too far into the realm of truth to turn back. Those who arrive here cannot return to their past. You can only move forward to the full Heaven of your holiness. For you the only the way forward is to Heaven, on the path of beautiful love. That is the road we have been traveling together for some time.

Now we begin a new phase in the journey of your soul, the phase of free expression of the limitlessness of love. A call has sounded in your heart and a voice in your mind. This heartbeat is not equal to others for it is God's call to Her beloved child. Your spirit yearns for freedom. The call of love cries out for unlimited expression. Incessantly Christ is calling you to bear witness to the truth.

These words will help you if you understand that they are a means and not an end. By joining them they are a means by which you can more vividly experience the sacred love you feel for me and the love I feel for you. By becoming more aware of the real love that exists between us, you allow love to manifest.

You will, without doubt, see the living expression of your self. The love given you from all eternity will be extended. You will do your work, which is God's work in you. It will be the perfect manifestation of that aspect of Divine Love that only you can express.

No one can love for another. In the same way, you cannot, nor should you try to, love as others love. Love with the heart that I gave you and you will be truly loving. Love with all your heart but love in your own way. Express yourself with the sincerity of your self, but do it your way.

V. Your Way of Loving

Love has infinite forms in which it manifests, because it is infinite. Each petal of each flower, each rose, each deer and antelope, each bird of the sky, and each human being, is a form of God's love made real in the physical world. In them, and in everything created, God is expressing Herself. Remember that it is proper for every self to express itself. This is why we take time now to speak of the expression of your heart. If you do not express yourself freely you cannot be full.

Free expression is essential to every self wishing to be free. No other definition of freedom can be more accurate than this. If you do not express love for God, you cannot express love at all, because God is love. To love God is to love life, and to love life is to love yourself. That is why, once again, we return to the source—which is to love God above all things. By letting yourself be loved by Her, by receiving Her love directly, then you can let your self fill to the point of overflowing, spilling over into the whole world.

We repeat again and again the need you have to let yourself love, because you have been living life feeling that you are not worthy of anything good, much less of God's love. The cruel and senseless belief that you were created to live a temporary life is so limiting that you have no idea of its damage. However, that belief has already been abandoned. No traces of it remain. Now we are becoming aware of the new self that you are. You are recognizing the beauty of who you really are.

There is no need to look back. Now we look only at the present through the eyes of love. We begin to glimpse our mission. We begin to see with clear vision. We begin to realize that all we need do is express what the depths of our self, both in the heart and mind, feel and think.

We have seen what our true heart wears and the holy ways of our Divine Mind. We have reached the Heart of God where we are one with the reality of love. We dwell in the abode of Christ. We live in the uncreated truth. We are the eternal reality of love expressing itself again and again. We are light that illuminates when we are what we really are.

We are God Herself every time we stop being what we thought we were but were not. We are one with our Mother. Together we are the Sacred Heart of Jesus and the Immaculate Heart of Mary living eternally in a unity without beginning or end. We are the love of the most Holy Trinity extending eternally. We are the light of the world.

The word has become flesh in us; in this way Christ returns to Earth in you.

Beloved of all times and places, until the word is necessary, it will continue to incarnate and manifest itself in time. I will never leave you. I will be with you until the end of time. I am the living word made a human reality. I am the living expression of love, just as you are.

Go around the world announcing the good news. Go tell the nations that Christ has arrived. Go to every corner, bringing the peace that I have given you. Go extend the love that lives in your heart. Live always in the presence of love.

There will be a time when words come to an end. At that time you will live eternally in the communion that comes from the language of love. Love has no words.

15.

Harvest Time

A message from the Voice of Christ through a Choir of Angels,
in the presence of Archangel Raphael and Archangel Gabriel

I. Prelude

Sons and daughters of Heaven! Holy reality of love made human!

If you were willing to recognize the absolute truth about all Creation, including yourself, you would eternally sing of the joy of being. Jubilantly would you recognize yourself as a personified miracle.

Beloveds of all corners of the universe, friends of God and of angels, friends of everything holy, beautiful, and perfect, at this time in the history of humanity we speak to you in all languages and in all corners of the Earth.

Forget not that you live in the times of the return to a direct relationship with God. When you see with the eyes of love, you can see expressions of God's love everywhere.

Today, beloved daughters and sons, we come to share good news through these words which are a unique expression of God's love. Share it with your sisters and brothers in Christ so that this chain of light spreads until it envelops the whole world.

Listen to our message with joy.

The fruits of the seeds of the Second Advent are appearing on all sides, seeds that the Sower has been sowing since Earth was conceived in the mind of the Creator, seeds that gave the sublime fruit of the incarnate Christ. The Tree of Life sprouts from wherever you who receive these words are.

Remember that love is the vine from which you grow as blessed branches, always beautiful, always holy, because of the wisdom that flows through your being. Love is your food. Remember also that you are the blessed fruit of Mary's womb, a plentiful fruit, pure and holy. You are the children of holiness, children of light.

Pure souls, born of divine beauty! We remind you that since time began, the First and Second Comings of Love were conceived as an indivisible unity. Love has never abandoned you and will never forsake you.

II. The Harvest Begins

Harvest time has arrived! A time of joy without equal! Truly, truly, we tell you that in some hearts green shoots have begun to germinate. Beautiful buds of holiness! Small flashes of light that, like fireflies in the night, with simplicity, fill creation with beauty while others sleep. These buds will grow as never before. Nothing can stop their flowering. They will become as beautiful, fruitful, and majestic as the One that gives them life.

In some places these seeds have grown so much that they are already beautiful acacias with abundant fruit. Many are eating this fruit, feeding souls, strengthening themselves in love. Some are sheltered as in a greenhouse. Others rest in the shadow and revel in their beauty.

Let the Earth be glad! Harvest time has arrived, a time of joy without equal.

You who receive these words, begin to contemplate the Earth from a new perspective, based on the wisdom of God. Look at Her with ecstatic eyes of love, love Her with a heart in love with Christ. Love Her with the heart that God gave you.

Extend your mind and your imagination beyond even the imaginable. Observe how a mighty river of living water flows without ceasing, bathed in the light of holiness, whose source is beyond what your eyes can see. Observe everything with the eyes of spirit. Begin to see the world through the vision of Christ.

Souls in love, we are here by your side, united by the eternal holiness that you are. Immerse yourself now with us in contemplating the flow of this river of love, a flow of serene waters, crystalline and beautiful, which waters in all directions, flowing from the source of eternal life, flooding the whole Earth with holiness. Can you hear the melodies that the waters sing as they slide down the channels of souls? It is the spirit of God, pouring forth ceaselessly in human spirits as never before in history.

The joy of Heaven is unparalleled. The beauty of your being has reached such a degree that even the most exalted of artists could not portray it, for it surpasses all imagination.

Brothers and sisters, the waters of eternal life are flowing from bank to bank, watering Earth with the love of God. They give life to everything they touch. They water the seeds that Christ himself has sown in union with us, the angels, and with you, the chosen ones of the Lamb, those who have made the fundamental choice for love.

This vision is a perfect representation of what is happening in your world. Even though not everyone can yet become conscious, humanity is being bathed more and more in an unfathomable ocean of perfect love.

Live joyfully in the certainty of love. Live in a way that the world has not yet taught you, but that can surely be lived.

III. A New Way of Living

The world is innocuous. It has never had any real effect on your being. Do not be afraid of the world, for it is already defeated, not in the sense of it being an enemy, but in that it has been transcended and reintegrated into the Kingdom of Heaven. Remember, your Kingdom is not of this world, but can extend into it. The world resides within the love that God is, since love encompasses everything.

The world of time is temporary, but it need not be cruel and loveless. Maybe it has been, but it need not remain so. If there is something that is clear about the world, it is that everything changes. It is a kingdom in which everything has its time.

In a world of time, everything has a beginning and an end through which transformation can take place. In a world of time, there is space for change, which is why everything changes.

Do not believe that the world has any power over your being. It never did, except when you wanted to play the game of granting it some power. We say "game" because in truth you cannot give your power to anyone or anything. Your power belongs to you and nothing and no one can take it from you, not even God.

What God gives is given eternally. In this lies the certainty of peace.

There is a time for everything: a time to give and a time to receive; a time to till the earth; a time to sow, a time to harvest, and a time to enjoy the harvest.

For everything there is a time, just as in breathing. There is a time to receive the breath and a time to give it. Without both movements, the life of the body would be impossible. Giving and receiving are one. There cannot be one without the other.

You cannot live life solely receiving or solely giving. Love is received and given in order to continue to be received and given. This is the rhythm of the dance of life. The law of giving and receiving as a unit is always respected. In time, you first receive, then you give. That is how the sequence manifests in time.

If for centuries the time of sowing has occurred, it is a sign that the harvest may come in your time. Brother, sister, the time is now—this very moment, wherever you are, whatever you are or think you are. The time of harvest has arrived. It has come for you and for the whole world.

Today, not yesterday, you can begin to live in a way that your being feels more and more comfortable, even in the world. Until now you had conceived the world as an unnatural place, with you being somehow an alien on Earth. Something in you did not fit with this world. Like a foreigner, you tried to adapt to a strange world. Like a fish out of water, you wasted your strength without achieving a fit in place, time, or circumstance. Is not it true that you have had this feeling?

What is it all about?

It is about you now becoming aware that your life can change completely once again —and every day —from an unnatural life to an ever-growing harmony with what you really are. Remember: you are reborn every day, a new creation.

Wake up every morning and remember that what you used to be has departed, never to return. Let it go. Make it a habit to live this new way, every day living this new life that love has prepared for you, for yesterday has gone and will never return.

It is not true that because you live in the world of matter, space, and time, you must live wrapped in the cloud of forgetfulness.

Listen to the good news! There is a way of living in the world that is in perfect harmony with your being. It exists. To begin to go through it you need but accept that it can only be known with the One who created you.

Everyone is unique. None are identical. Some are more similar than others but none are identical. God loves diversity and does not clone.

Express your own way to be in truth and not in illusion, for that enables you to live in harmony with what you are. Does this not make sense? How could you express yourself freely in harmony with what you are if what you were doing is based on a mind that does not know who you really are? Can the intellect know God directly?

Only the living Christ who lives in you can know your perfect path. This is not a matter of rules or commandments but a matter of harmony. Would God create a beautiful hummingbird with the impetus to fly and not give everything necessary for that impulse to come true? The birds are happy flying, the fish swimming, and the daisies receiving the sun, rain, and all the love of God. What of you?

When the Earth you step onto and the air you breathe was conceived, perfect paths were also conceived so that beings could live temporarily.

Your life in space-time has a beginning and an end. That path takes you, little by little, back to the Heaven of your Sacred Heart. The path waiting for you has as its function the expression of your holiness.

You have made a discovery. You have discovered that you are, in humility, the Christ of God. You have received that message. God knows who you really are and you know the Christ that lives in you. Now that you know, it is time for the harvest, the time in which Christ must be for you like a serene river that runs gently but firmly, carrying the calm waters to your soul, your being, your mind, and your heart. The Christ knows what is natural to your being, even within the world.

To live in such a way that only Christ lives in you, leaving aside any pattern of thought and emotional response not His, is what we speak of. It may seem unacceptable or difficult, but we assure you it is the easiest path in the world. And the happiest.

Listen once again. The way you will know if you are walking the path that Christ has dreamed for you in the world is this: All walking will be easy, effortless, devoid of the fear of uncertainty; a happy path, full of meaning, so easy for you that one day you will realize that you are letting yourself be carried along by the calm waters of the love that lives in you.

Let yourself go. You will see your life change, and with it the life of the world. Once again we say: Renounce the past. Throw yourself confidently into the arms of love. Start now to live a new life, the life of the living Christ that lives in you. Let that holy confluence of your mind and heart, which you call Christ, be the only source of your knowledge and action. Then you will be saying Yes to life. How? Remember or say:

I no longer live. It is Christ who lives in me.

16.

A New Beginning

A message from Jesus, identifying himself as
"the living Christ who lives in you"

I. Prelude

Sons and daughters of inextinguishable light! We are clothed with pure love to dwell with you in the presence of the holiness that you are in truth. You are holy because God is holy. You are beautiful because God is beauty itself. What a joy to have arrived together at this time without equal, a time full of blessings and divine Grace.

You are tired. You have traveled winding roads to arrive at this point. Lay your head on my shoulders. Let me caress your hair. I invite you to rest in my heart and to shelter your being. Let me fill you with peace.

Beloved of the Creator, the time for planting is over. The time of harvest has arrived. Be happy. Begin to relax and live serenely. Little by little you will feel more comfortable in these lands of peace and endless harmony. They are different from the territory you once knew, but they are what your heart has desired. Do not be afraid. We are always by your side. United we are the light of the world. Together we are invincible, for the strength of love lies in our unity.

We are speaking of living in times that are no longer those of sowing. Remember, Christ is the sower; the harvest is His gift of love for you. You receive, you give.

The "living Christ that lives in you" is simply an expression that tries to name that part of you capable of uniting Heaven and Earth. That part of you is real. It is the reality of love that has become your identity. Everything that belongs to God belongs to you.

The living Christ who lives in you is that part of God that extends to you and keeps in your being all that is divine and human, because your humanity, as well as your divinity, belongs to God. Remember that the outside world is not separate from the inside world, just as Earth is not separate from Heaven; these are two aspects of the same unique reality, the reality of love. There is no separation.

Your humanity and your divinity are not two different realities that come together in a relationship. They are one. As you progress in the discernment of truth, you recognize that a relationship and its parts are one and the same. There are no separate parts in a holy relationship. Thus the name of the most Holy Trinity has been given as, "Father, Son, and the Spirit of love that unites them in an eternal holy relationship." We have already discussed this, but we recall it now because it is necessary to remember that the path of life is already the path of beautiful love.

There is no reason to wait to begin living consciously in the reality of love. You are the reality of love. My son, my daughter, you are living in the reality of God.

Just as you were told that the world has long since ceased to exist, the same goes for your return to love: it has been a while since you returned. Since long, long ago, you are the living expression of love extending eternally in everything and everyone. Perhaps this is not perceived as true, because perception is subject to time and sees everything as a logical sequence of "if this, then that." Thus thinks the mind: "If I am still in the world, then I am not in Heaven." Such thought patterns exist, and now we abandon that patterned thinking. We let it go without judging anything.

Even long before My voice manifested itself in this way for you to hear—and all those who receive these words hear it—came signs that you are not of the world, despite being in it.

You are the Christ of God who has returned to Earth in your true identity. Accepting this as true for you and making this truth the nourishment of your life is what it means to accept the harvest. Christ sows. Christ harvests. Christ is.

The harvest is abundant. Day after day you will see its manifestation in your life. You will walk the path that your being longs for, because what you long for in the depths of your soul is what God longs for in you.

From now on you can travel the roads of the world without being a stranger in a strange land. Souls are not alien to you. Your sisters and brothers are not alien to you. The beings that inhabit the Earth are not alien to you. Now that you see with the vision of Christ, you recognize the truth in each being, which is why you can live in the world without losing yourself in it.

II. The Treasures of Being

You will be what you should be. You will be the Christ of God, awakening your sisters and brothers with your single existence, along with all beings that inhabit Earth. Your radiance does not come from the thinking mind, which is not the living Christ. You illuminate by the mere fact of being, because you are true light. You are a being of light.

You will increasingly unify with children of light according to the law of attracting that which is alike. Love attracts love, light attracts holiness. Where light exists, darkness cannot. Children of light are already enlightened, just as you are; do not judge their different ways of enlightening.

Remember that fireflies, stars, and the sun all illuminate in their own manner. Each give beauty merely by being what they really are. Children of light are the saviors of the world. Without them there would be no hope that the physical universe would return to the love of God. These children of holiness are reborn from the spirit of God for the salvation of the whole world.

They are the co-creators of the Second Advent. They have accepted holiness for themselves, not because they have won it in some way, but because in humility they recognized that holiness is the gift of God for all, and they have received it with joy in their hearts. They are those who love themselves as God loves them.

Beauty of Heaven! Your thinking mind is a blessing from God, an ineffable gift of love, as is everything that comes from the Creator. Honor your mind, let it serve what it was created for: to be a blessed mirror of divine truth, the abode of wisdom, a sacred temple where the sweetness of love dwells.

Brother, sister, you were also given a heart that allows you to do what it always knows how to do, that for which it was created. Allow it to be a pure vessel where love overflows to such an extent that it floods the Earth with its peace, beauty, and holiness. You have a heart for love. Honor it as the treasure of Christ, the temple of God.

You have been given a spirit capable of holding both mind and the heart, united with will and memory. This union is similar to God.

Soul in love, with so many treasures received, with so much beauty given, how could you not be the perfect reflection of the Christ of God? Christ lives in you. Christ is what you really are.

You need no longer strive to know who you are. What sense would that make, now that you know what you are? You need no longer fight to try to show what you never were nor could be. You need no longer fight for survival. Why would you believe that you need to survive what is eternal?

Harvest time has arrived. What you have sought has in truth been given to you in holiness, deposited in your mind and heart, united in a divine unity.

We tell you clearly what the living Christ is that lives in you so that you do not get lost on the path to truth on which you already travel, and to protect you from ramblings that have no relationship to the will of God. What you are has the inherent capacity to express itself and always has. Therefore worry not about what the expression of the living Christ living in you will be like.

Just as water that fills a container assumes its form, so God's creation fills your soul and adopts your way of being. In this way God Who has no attributes takes on attributes, a process by which love takes form. This is what happens in you. We have called this metanoia, or conversion.

III. Fruit of Planting

A harvest consists of collecting the fruits of the sowing, in this case, the fruit of love. The way this fruit germinates in you is unique. In the Garden of Eden that is expressed in all souls, no flower is the same as another, even though all are perfect expressions of the same love.

Remember that what you were looking for was really looking for you. And since what you really wanted was love, that is, your being, then your being, which never left you, found you first. This is not a play on words; it is the reality of spiritual life.

You are not a body. You know that. You are much more than that. You are a human spirit, created by God, with the ability to create worlds. From the inner world arises the outer world. From an inner world without love, a world arises without love; from an inner world full of love, a world full of love emerges.

Herein lies the answer to all your questions. Did you ever sin? No. You just stopped filling yourself with love, and thereby emptied yourself of your being. Did you ever hate? No. You simply blocked the reception of love from your consciousness, leaving your consciousness empty of the recognition of the love that you are.

What you are never stopped being you. Neither did your true consciousness, which is the consciousness of Christ. In Christ consciousness resides the knowledge of self.

Christ knows its own consciousness. God knows Herself in Her own consciousness. This is always the case: being knows its own consciousness. It is not that consciousness creates knowledge, but that the being has deposited in consciousness part of what is. And since there is only one true consciousness, that is, Divine consciousness, then only in God can you really know yourself.

Everything is given by God. Nothing is not given by God. What She does not give does not exist. Who would create it? You may argue that God does not give cars or houses or material things such as money, phones, and harps. That is true, but who gave you the material to make those things? Who gave you the mind capable of making them?

What you are is the work of God. Accept everything as a gift of your loving will because it is so. Remember that what you sought with all your heart found you first. Otherwise you could not have looked for it with all your heart.

The life you want is calling you. This abundant life, full of meaning, joy, and lasting peace, resides within you. Let it manifest more every day. Remember that love is infinite and always creates more love.

Stay connected to that part of you where the Heavens reside in Their totality and you will see how everything that happens in your life will be holy. No matter what arises within the framework of your consciousness, everything will shine in the light of Christ.

The issue is not to avoid the problems of the world, but not to get lost in them. Remember again that life is neutral; what is not neutral is your way of seeing it, your interpretation of it. The mind and heart are never neutral, because the power of thought causes everything to have an effect on some level.

If you fear something that may happen from time to time, be not scared or self-judgmental. You are no less spiritual if you feel panic or feel useless to do something your heart asks of you. None of that matters.

It is not about living in such a way that you do not feel fear, but that you do not allow fear to paralyze you. You can live fully in love and perfectly walk the path in harmony with your being even in the midst of fear. The day will come when it will end.

You are not being called to be a brave warrior who advances where no one in his right mind would in order to demonstrate his superiority even at the cost of his life. We are not looking for heroes. We are not looking for anything. We are love extending.

What you are being asked, out of love, is that as you walk together in harmony with our being, that you open yourself to embrace everything that arises within the love of our being. Remember that you are simply experiencing human life, but now you do so with the purpose of being who you really are.

Truly we tell you that where one day you lost yourself, you will now find yourself. Fear will no longer cause unrest. You will only want to live in the harmony of your being. You will recognize that the closer you get to love, the less you want its opposite. You will not want anything other than peace and harmony, the result of union.

Love your vulnerability. Love your weakness, your fragility, your limitations. Love also every time you experience your immensity, your boundless vastness, your irresistible power. Love the fact that you are all this and much more. Love everything that arises inside you.

Begin now to travel this new path with us, the countless angels of Heaven and the bearers of the voice of Christ, in union with all creation. This way expresses more each day the love that you truly are, in your particular way. This is a call to immerse yourself more and more deeply in truth, a call to travel the path of love, the path of being that God created to be you.

17.

The Power of Silence

A message from Jesus, identifying himself as "the living Christ who lives in you"

I. The Return to the World

As you traverse the plains, after having "descended" from the top of the mountain, you will experience new things. It is important that you be aware of some of them. In reality you already know them, because for a long time the spirit of wisdom has taken you to the mountaintop and spoken to your heart, and in those dialogues of love, you became aware of the being that you truly are.

You were raptured, literally enraptured in spirit and truth. You were taken to the peaks of Heaven and from there you saw panoramas of the universe, including those of the world of time and space from God's perspective. This is not a metaphorical expression. It is the truth about the path of your soul, and of all souls who have come this far. Dear one, the rapture of the soul exists.

You knew that the return to the plain would not be easy. Once you have tasted the sweetness of God's love, tasted the honey of your wisdom, and vividly experienced the tenderness of your unwavering peace, who would want to return to a world in which the light of truth does not shine, nor does it rest in the arms of love? And yet, we went down to the plain. We descended once more to the world. For what?

If you do not know the purpose of your return to the life of the world after having had the experience of the Kingdom, the path becomes rough. But if you adhere to your purpose, you will begin to live with much more serenity and ease.

There is a feeling that we must come to the light and unite with it. That feeling is related to the return from the mountaintop. That is what we will speak of in this session of love and truth.

Once you have found yourself, you will never want to stop living in union with the living Christ that you are. You have found the pearl of great price, the hidden treasure. You have found yourself, joined your being. Now you are the realized one. You are the one who has found. You are the enlightened one. In short, you are.

This feeling is the aftertaste of the transcendence of mundane things, arising from the value you have found in the eternal. The world stops having intrinsic value to those who know Heaven. No one who has left the world and returned to God's Heaven has the slightest intention of returning to the experience of human life. The life of opposites had no meaning to those who know a reality that has no opposite.

So what is the point of returning to the world? Why did I return after my forty days and forty nights in the desert? For the same reason you did. Remember, you and I travel the same path.

Because I knew that you would find certain parts of the path difficult, I gave you my gospels. They reveal a lot about the challenges I had to face in my public ministry: conflicts, diatribes, invasive behaviors, anxieties of all kinds, not to mention the anger that was almost always present.

II. Extended Consciousness

Truly, not a single day in my public life was free of difficulty. Observing this led me to say: "Do not worry about what you will eat tomorrow or how you will dress. Each day has its sorrows and joys."

This is true not only for those who have returned from the top of the mountain, but for all. Yet for those who savored the sweetness of beautiful love, it is experienced in a different way.

It is not that the world rises up against you because you have returned; it is that now your degree of consciousness does not allow you to ignore the slightest strand of truth. You do not deny anything anymore. You live in the reality of what you are. You embrace each feeling for what it is. You do not try to give a false name to a feeling or try to reject what you clearly feel—whether joy, pain, anger, enthusiasm, discouragement, hope, vitality, depression. In short, the color palette of emotions unfolds in all its expressions.

My beloveds! For what else would you be enraptured and taken to Heaven, where we love and speak in the deepest intimacy of our being, but that we can begin to walk the path of the heart together?

I did not touch your heart "just because." You gave it to me. And I made it one with mine. Now we are one holy heart, a single true being. When I put my finger on the center of your being, your soul was ecstatic. Your mind was submerged in the reality of love in an indivisible union with your heart. You became one in yourself and one with me. From the integrity of all that you are, you joined my divinity. This is how the new being that you are was born.

The path of the heart, which is the one that all those who receive these words are called to travel, does not simply ask you to accept everything that you experience within yourself and embrace it in your consciousness. It is a path that leads you to walk in truth. It is a path of deep honesty with yourself, and consequently with others, with the world, and with God.

Honesty is essential to your being because you cannot live in any reality other than the truth. Deceiving, denying, and evading were mental and emotional mechanisms of the ego. Those patterns are what the path of the heart dismantles and deprograms.

You have returned to the plain of the world with your heart wide open. This has made you much more sensitive than before. When you opened your heart, love came to dwell in you.

With a sensitive heart, we must now walk through a world about which we previously were discouraged. With a mind imbued with wisdom not of the world, we must tread where we previously perceived ignorance. We know that this world cannot give what only God can give.

III. The Mundane and the Spiritual

Why travel the path of the heart in this world? Why were you not taken instead to other dimensions where there is the beauty, harmony, peace, and happiness that your heart longed for? How long before we are finally together in our Heaven?

These questions remain in the depths of a mind attached to a heart when it returns from the mountain of God down to the plains of human experience. These questions denote a tension between the mundane and the celestial, between the human and the divine.

We begin by accepting that tension. Observe your body and soul, and you may feel that tension. It may even be so strong that you develop physical illnesses. This is no longer the tension of the past, between the ego and God. It is the tension between living in the world and being of it and living in the world and not being of it, and the possibility of completely abandoning mundane reality to live definitively in the Kingdom of Heaven where you know you dwell eternally.

These tensions will pass. They are the manifestation of the feelings of rejection that your being naturally develops to everything that does not come from the eternal reality of love. You would like to flee to the mountain and disconnect from the world. You would like to seclude yourself so that nothing distracts you from our direct relationship. In short, we have called this feeling the desire to get out of life.

The path of the heart is one of deep honesty. Henceforth you must accept that life is now your teacher in a new way: Now, for you, life is God. Now you realize that when I said I was life, I was not speaking metaphorically. What does this mean? It means that every event of your life on this path of the heart is the perfect means that your Mother uses to transform you, more and more, into what She and only She has for you. Now life itself is the great teacher, the shaper, not of your personality, but of you. I shall clarify.

Experience is perception because it is its cause. Cause and effect are one. You might argue that it makes no sense to live a life that molds you if your being is immutable and you do not need to be molded into the real you. You might also say in truth, although in part, that perception is not necessary in Heaven, for there one enjoys perfect knowledge. All of this is true. But it is also true that it is necessary to deprogram perception to the point where holy perception leads to the recognition that no perception is necessary. Simply put, collective and individual thought patterns and emotional responses must be dismantled.

Your mind and your heart are united with the collective mind and heart. For this reason it is always necessary to return to the plain. I told this to my beloved apostles on Mount Tabor. The life you experience is the perfect medium for memories out of harmony with God to be erased, reprogrammed, and emptied of everything untrue. In this way you receive the memory of God. We could say that the events of life on the plain are the perfect means for you to forget the world and remember God.

I said that the way of the heart consists of walking in truth. In this sense it is the path of humility. It is a way in which you do not seek to modify anything—not the world, not the events that come to you, not the people, not yourself. We only seek to gather everything that arises in our interior. We accept that God knows what the events, things, and characters are that must act together so that this process of memory healing occurs.

IV. Perfect Love Consciousness

Just as God Herself took us from the state of spiritual amnesia to the state of Christ Consciousness in which we now live, She will also take us to the state of the fullness of being or the consciousness of perfect love.

The world is now the perfect medium for the chrysalis to become a butterfly and for it to know how to fly.

In this path of the heart it is essential to accept everything you feel, think, or experience inside without trying to label it, name it, or decide anything about it. This path is not about doing but about feeling. Feeling is the key word. Remember that the fear of feeling is basic. It is present in all fears because ultimately fear is a denial of being and you deny your being by not feeling what your being feels.

In the way of the heart, when you feel anger, you say to yourself: "I feel anger. I do not like how I feel, but it is what I feel. I allow myself to feel every drop of anger that has come to me. I will not do anything with it except to feel it in all its breadth and width." If what emerges is joy, we accept joy and feel it. We do not try to label it, nor say that it is better than other emotions. We just feel every drop of joy as we did with anger, or as we do with the deepest sadness or the greatest pleasure.

The key is to feel. Why? Because it is through your emotions and feelings that the process of transformation is taking place and means to complete it. Remember that in feelings as well as in thoughts is life. Remember also that we no longer make a separation between thinking and feeling, but take them as a unit. Both are aspects of a single reality, the reality of your soul.

When we emphasize feeling, we do not do so to put aside what you think. We do it because the fear of feeling has been much greater than the fear of thinking, although both exist within the palette of fears you have experienced.

The fear of insanity can be as intense as the fear of losing control of your emotions. This must not be forgotten. Both fears are unfounded. However, merely by saying that these fears are illusory does not accomplish much. You need to experience this truth. You need to experience how, when certain thoughts or emotions arise that you previously denied out of fear, they have no real effect on you. Life now will bring you situations to dismantle your fears. And you will see that it works.

An essential aspect of this path through the plain, which you walk with your heart in your hand, is to become an inseparable friend of silence. You will experience its transforming and miraculous power.

Before, when you experienced something you did not like, you reacted more or less with anger. You manifested that anger either outwardly or inwardly. You will no longer do so. Now you will simply remain with silent feeling. At the outset you may feel as if you are standing in front of the cross as I am being crucified. Maybe you can withstand this mystical experience, or maybe you cannot. It does not matter. What matters is that you keep every drop of feeling and thought in the silence of your heart.

V. Divine Silence

We now speak of the power of silence and its importance to you. In silence everything becomes one with God. In silence is where metanoia happens, the coal becomes a diamond. Silence is the divine matrix in which everything is born. Silence is an aspect of divine nothingness.

In the stillness everything is born. Therefore if you take your emotions into the silence of your heart and allow them to be as they are, you will see them being born, growing, and then disappearing. They are like waves in water, like a musical note that is born out of silence and then vanishes.

If you exercise the power of silence you will see, little by little, that all power returns to you. Many times the external expression of emotions is but the desire to dissipate their energy. Now we no longer do that, but we let any energy that appears in our soul be as it is. We do not think anything about it, whether an emotion, a feeling, or a thought. We do not identify with anything.

In every feeling, emotion, or thought that arises inside you is a message of love, as well as in every event of your life. The circumstances of your daily life help you elicit the emotions, thoughts, and feelings that you experience.

The messages that events bring cannot be understood in words nor put into thoughts. Their language is not the language of the thinking mind.

The message of feelings, emotions, and thoughts is in the energy of each. Some bring the energy of fear, others of love. What they bring can only be appreciated if you allow each one to be integrated into your consciousness as it is. But you must feel them. And you cannot feel them in their fullness if you are not silent, focusing your gaze on your soul, and allowing everything to be felt.

This is not about trying to understand, but about allowing everything to come to you without resistance—no matter if what comes is the strength of an anger that you feel to be devastating, or a disgust that makes your stomach turn, or a calm and peaceful feeling.

Practice the power of silence. Allow yourself to feel everything you feel and to experience everything that you experience without doing anything about it except to feel and absorb every drop of its energy. If you do this, you will be lord of a spiritual practice as powerful as any other, the power of metanoia. In addition, with this practice you intertwine the path of the heart with the path of transformation and that of knowledge. The union of these three paths is what we call the path of the wisdom of the heart. Through the power of silence you perform miracles for yourself and others. In peace you create a new Heaven and a new Earth. By remaining in the silence of your heart you are the perfect expression of the power of love.

18.

Alchemy

A message from Jesus, identifying himself as
"the living Christ who lives in you"

I. The Path of Transformation

Being an alchemist is part of your function. An essential but rarely recognized power within you, or rather within creation, is the power of transformation. That power, arising from the silence of the heart where it resides, is what makes everything in the world of form capable of being transformed. This power is inherent in form, and comes from your being. The being that God is carries within Herself that power. Otherwise form could not have it.

The true power of silence lies not in speaking much or little, or making much or little noise, but in attention. It is a matter of consciousness. Mindfulness can only be achieved in a soul that has made silence its faithful friend and has developed a conscious love relationship with it.

If there is anything you acquired at the top of the mountain, it is the awareness that within you is a silent space as sacred as the most venerated temple on Earth. That core of your being, that silence in which you are fully yourself, that nothingness in which everything arises, is what we call the silence of the heart.

In that space, the center of your being, resides all the power of God, and therefore of creation.

To live centered is to live connected with that silent space of your heart, your being. Whenever you move out of that silence you suffer because you have ceased to be aware of who you are. That silence is your being. It is that in you wherein resides all the power and glory of Heaven and Earth. There is no other place where this power resides, nor where it can manifest itself, except in the silence of your heart.

I assure you that the power that lives in the silence of your being is so overwhelming compared to the power of the world, that before it every army would fall apart were they able to see it. They do not see it because silence encompasses sounds, images, touch, and everything else that can be perceived by the bodily senses.

Since the senses of the body cannot enter that arena of pure silence, of nothingness, then the thinking mind cannot understand it. That is why we take sequential steps in your spiritual path. First you had to dis-identify yourself from your thoughts, and then from your feelings and emotions. Once you have achieved this, you can gather all that you are and take it to the silence of your being where it is transformed by love into greater loving consciousness.

II. A New Purpose

The life you live now, after the "descent" from the mountaintop, is what allows you to grow in awareness. It is the perfect means to broaden your heart in the awareness of love. You become more conscious as you wake from Adam's dream. Your spiritual amnesia heals.

All these descriptions will help you better understand the path on which you travel, and your purpose.

We said earlier that where you encountered fear you will now find security, and where you experienced separation you will experience unity. In order to become aware of this, it is necessary to take everything within you to that holy place.

Think of the silence of the heart like a place in your soul where there is nothing. Imagine nothingness. It is vibrant, full of unmanifested life. It is so immense that the physical universe is for it like a small nut placed in the palm of its hand. Begin to conceive of silence and vastness as a space without beginning or end. There is space for everything.

Stillness and emptiness are the reality of God. There is nothing in Her, yet within that nothingness resides the vibrant, pure potentiality of infinite totality. Thus God is everything, including nothingness.

Feel the vibrant force of that place of absolute silence. There are no sounds and no images—only one energy that vibrates incessantly. It is the matrix of your being, created in the likeness of the Creator. Within it resides all creative power. Feel it. Do not label it.

Stay in silence now for a moment no matter where you are or what you are doing.

Feel every fiber of the physical body. Each breath. Every heartbeat. Observe each thought silently. Feel whatever comes up. Listen to everything that can be heard around you. Savor every wisp of wind. Smell every aroma.

Begin to perceive the silence that exists between each sound, the space between each object, the absence of aromas when they have returned to nothing or when they have not yet emerged. Focus your attention on the nothingness that surrounds you everywhere. Nothing. Silence. Expectation. Emptiness. Empty of everything and everyone.

Be silent. You are in the temple where She Who has no name resides. Breathe. Rest well. Be quiet. Observe. Wait. Stay.

III. The Memory of the First Love

As you practice the power of silence, which you already know well how to do, the memory of the love you experienced at the top of the mountain remains in your consciousness. Walking through the world centered in the silence of your heart, you are called to live as an impartial observer and to quietly look and wait within the shelter of your being. This way of living, so different from the way of living in the world, will manifest the power of your heart.

Remember that we are not advocating the non-expression of feelings, emotions, or thoughts; we are advocating the power of love and its necessary relationship with truth. To live in truth is to live consciously in the truth of everything that is happening in your inner world.

The Kingdom consists of ideas, memories, thoughts, desires, emotions, feelings, intuitions, and many other things. It is the realm to which the consciousness of every place, time, and circumstance must be brought for the alchemy of your soul to be completed.

If you do not express your feelings, you repress a part of your being. However, not all external expression, as you conceive it, is a true expression. True expressions of who you are arise from the wisdom of love, and she gives herself to you in the silence of your heart. If you express yourself from a place where truth does not reside, your expression will be an illusion.

But if you express yourself from the center of your being, your expression will be reliable. That truthful expression will, first, make your perception trustworthy, and then unnecessary. It will have you live in the knowledge of who you really are. This is why we have said that the path of the heart is linked to both transformation and knowledge. There is only one place where they meet and intertwine: in the sacred silence of your soul, your heart.

When you remain in your heart and hold everything there, you will know what to do or what not to do, what to say or not say, and everything you express will be in harmony with your being. It will not arise from social, moral, religious, or similar conditioning. It will be your own answer. Remember that the events that seem to arise before your eyes are in themselves nothing; the only value therein is in the true response that you give.

IV. All or Nothing

One of the central transformations that this process of spiritual alchemy performs—and please pay attention—is the following.

When you take everything to the center of your being and immerse it in the silence of your heart, allowing yourself to experience whatever you experience, you will begin to know true discernment. Such discernment does not arise from the thinking mind but from your being. It does not necessarily need to be expressed in words or sounds, for remember that love has no words.

This is the only discernment called for. What is not love is fear. What is fear is nothing. What is love is everything. Only love is real. Nothing unreal exists.

Begin to realize that all you can experience is nothingness or everything, fear or love. This is the basis of your salvation. Would you fear what you truly recognize is nothing? Does it make sense to do anything with nothing?

Beloved brother, beloved sister, this is where we begin to become aware of and to disarticulate the memories that told us that fear was fearsome. Being afraid of fear is frightening for those who have not recognized fear as nothing.

The fear of fear can be eliminated from your experience forever. When you are told not to be afraid of anything, you are also told not to be afraid of feeling afraid. You are afraid to feel anger, rejection, anger, or anything else that you do not like precisely because you will never like nothingness.

You were created by the All of everything in its likeness. Therefore you are everything. The fear of experiencing sensations that would seem to disintegrate you inwardly leading to an absolute lack of control and loss of reason is a fear we must now release forever. In the silence of the heart, this release will be made of love for yourself.

Fear creates a state of panic in you now. Since you have known the peace of God, you now fear losing it and returning to the past. With your love of truth and thoughts of God you fear to fall again. Your hair stands on end and your muscles tense as if trying to hold your being from falling back.

The fear of falling is a fear of returning to the past, based on the idea that love can leave you because you think you have abandoned love. It is important to understand that this notion is false and to cease harboring it. You never abandoned love. You always wanted to be.

Love never abandons. Love is what you are. You cannot separate from it or it from you; otherwise you would cease to exist along with all creation. Even God would not exist if you did not exist, because you are God. You are being God when you live your life as God created you to be, as the love that you really are. "My Father and I are one," says the eternally living Christ who lives in you. "I do only the will of my Father," says your being forever, truthfully.

A pedagogical way to overcome the fear of fear is to go back and review situations where you experienced fear, not imagined fears but those in everyday life, and thereby to realize that they have no power over you. There has never been a time when fear, expressed in any form, has had any true effect on you. This you already know. You have already walked this path. You have progressed enough to realize that what is being said here is true.

Allow yourself now and always the power of spiritual alchemy. Bring everything to the silence of your heart. Resist nothing. Accept all as coming from God because that is the way it is. Thus little by little you will begin to transform memories of fear into those of love. You will have taken countless sisters and brothers out of hell. Once that is done, you will ascend to Heaven where together we will continue to love each other, creating new love eternally.

The ability to discern between what is nothing and what is everything is ultimately all the spiritual path is about, and is the basis of alchemy or metanoia. As we have said, this is not a matter of intellectual exercise but a matter of experiencing yourself in everything you are on all levels.

Now you can begin to think differently about anger or any murderous thought. You can say: "I'm experiencing nothing. I do not like it, but it's what I'm experiencing. I will allow myself to experience it. It has no real effect on me, but now I feel it and I encourage myself to feel it in its fullness."

This understanding of nothing and everything will help greatly from now on, since the word fear brings with it many attributes that no longer make sense and have increased your confusion. While this is part of the past, remember that we are healing memory. We are beginning to remember the state of pure love, a state in which fear does not exist, nor anything like it.

In the silence of your heart give everything to me and allow me to do or undo it. To weave a new web. To work miracles. You will learn that you perform miracles from that place of silence where you give everything to your being and allow yourself to occupy yourself. This is the definition of miraculous mentality: a mental state in which you take to the center of your being everything that arises, literally delivering it to the Christ in you and allowing Christ to resolve all things according to His divine approval. This is how you stop being intelligent and become wise: you allow the holy wisdom of God to be the source of your knowledge and action.

19.

The Wisdom of the Self

A message from Jesus, identifying himself as
"the living Christ who lives in you"

I. The Guided Self

Going from a life marked by intellectual knowledge—worldly knowledge—to that ruled by the wisdom of God is your goal and where we are now heading with certainty.

The wisdom of Heaven is inherent in being. When we speak of the wisdom of the heart it is about the wisdom of your being. Remember, the heart is the name we have given to the center of your being.

There was no need to dethrone the wisdom of Heaven from your soul and replace it with a strange mechanism of intellectual reasoning based on trial and error, and effort. Yet that is what happened. Now we recognize, first, that the wisdom of God exists. Then we recognize that it must dwell in some place or state.

We appeal to reason. She will tell us that everything created is imbued with wisdom. We accept once again the irrefutable fact of the great intelligence that gives order to everything, of the great creative power capable of creating souls, wills, hearts, thinking beings, irrational beings, and much more. We accept it because we see it. We do not deny the reality in front of us.

We already know for sure that God is love. Reason now tells us that love cannot have been left to itself but is accompanied by the wisdom that rules life and therefore our being. We know that love spares nothing. Love is eternally giving everything. We know that we are similar to our Creator. Thus we know that the wisdom of God, which is the wisdom of life, resides in every living being and in everything that has been called into being.

Ignorance is not what you have been created for. Wisdom is the natural state of being, and therefore of yourself. It is absurd to suppose even if you cannot hear the voice of the conscience of Christ that you would have to create a voice of a moral or social conscience.

The voice of Christ is the voice of wisdom because Christ is wisdom. You believed that the wise were those few who had been so graced, and did not know why their gift was one you lacked. Perhaps, with your sense of justice, you believed that God would not give to some what She does not give to all. But such a belief is not enough; it is necessary that you accept it for yourself. Even if you believe that God is fair and abundant, it may still be challenging to accept that She is fair with you in particular.

One of the problems you had with wisdom is the thought that it is something alien to you and that it had to be given to you. But wisdom is what you are. It cannot be defined in any other way since wisdom and love are one and the same. Remember that the only way to define love is that love is. Thus wisdom is.

II. Wisdom and Unity

There cannot be a being over here and wisdom over there. A being is necessarily a being of wisdom, for it is a being of love. You are not ignorant. You never were and never will be. None of your sisters and brothers are either. Neither are the other beings that inhabit the Earth alien to wisdom. You are the wisdom of God personified. You are love extending eternally.

The question is not whether you are ignorant, but whether you are aware of the wisdom of the love that lives in you. You can only be aware of your wisdom if you live life centered on your being and allow it to ask the questions, give the answers, and decide whether you need to act or not. This is a matter of practice.

You can deny the wisdom of your being, although not totally. This is the same as saying you can deny the voice of God, although never in its entirety. To deny your being means to deny love, truth, and wisdom. It also denies the treasures of the Kingdom.

When you denied your being, wisdom remained in a state of immanence, that is, it only acted for the basic issues of your existence. You cannot stop existing because what God creates is eternal. But you can reduce your light to such a point that it is only a tiny spark.

While it is true that this spark is more than enough to sustain your existence, it is also true that with it you do not have the awareness of the Christ that you are in truth. Thus although the light of Christ will always shine in you, your expression of it may not. That depends on your free will. That is the space of your will.

Denying the wisdom of God in you is a clear example of the denial of true knowledge. Knowing is a matter of direct relationship. In wisdom there is no process of elaboration. Either you know directly or you do not know at all. Either you know something with perfect certainty or you do not know.

Certainty, knowledge, and wisdom go hand in hand. Not knowing submerges you in ignorance, which, although not a state created by God, can be achieved. The same goes for guilt, because fear, guilt, and ignorance go hand in hand.

Although wisdom, like love, does not need words, it can be expressed in words if necessary. You cannot explain what wisdom is because to do so would explain what love is. Nobody can teach you to be wise, just as no one can teach you to love.

III. Wisdom, Relationship, and Miracles

Accessing the wisdom of love is something you do in direct relationship with God. This is the reason you are urged to exercise the power of silence more and more. In the silence of your heart the wisdom of Christ whispers to you with all the softness of love. In the midst of noise it is impossible to hear the voice of wisdom.

We wish to remind you, blessed soul of the Father, that there is a place in you where a sacred silence reigns, where the voice of the consciousness of Christ communicates with you and is not only able to inform you but to act or avoid acting. To allow this is to allow wisdom to be the source of your knowledge and action.

Knowing before acting is wise. What is not usually recognized is that wisdom informs, speaks, and takes action together. There is no sequence. This is the basis of miracles. Wisdom is the source of miracles.

What is being revealed to you is access to miracle-mindedness. Let us review the basic postulates so as to hold on to this forever.

You allow everything that arises in the plain of your life to be as it is. You dare to feel whatever you feel. You do not seek to change anything. You do not judge anything you experience. You watch, you wait. You experience everything life has for you. You let the thoughts and mental patterns be as the mind wants them to be; you leave them free.

Once everything that arises within your interior is accepted and embraced in the love that you are, you take everything to the silence of your heart. There you allow the power of silence to do what it does. You allow the alchemy of your thoughts, emotions, and feelings. Thus does being transform your memory, understanding, and will in the realm of consciousness. The wisdom of love begins to imbue everything you are.

Then in the silence of your being, you listen to Christ: "Do you give me your soul?" And you begin to know the beauty of divine mercy. Stay quiet. Watch and wait. Listen as your being tells the love that Christ is: "I give it all to you. You take care of everything. Show me what you want to show me. Act according to your divine pleasure. Thy will be done."

Then you wait. What has to be done will be done. What you have to say you will know to say without any doubt, as you will know when to be silent. It will be wisdom that acts for you and for others.

Certainly you can maintain a conscious dialogue with Christ at all times and in all places, just as you would with your dearest friend. You can ask him concretely to do this or that miracle for you. He will, because now you act from the wisdom of love and not from ignorance. Your whole being has been consciously given to God through the practice of the power of silence; the energy that you carry there is transmuted into love.

Truly, truly, I tell you that you have a right to miracles just as the bride and groom at the wedding of Cana did. Never believe there are limits to miracles. No miracle is small or large. All miracles are simply acts of love. And everything needs to receive the love of God.

Living constantly in miracle-mindedness is possible. It is the result of the transformation of which we speak. By changing false perception to reliable perception, you change from ego mentality to miracle mentality, or to the mind of Christ.

In truth you already live in miracle-mindedness. The only thing we are doing here is growing in the degree of awareness of it. Let this new mentality rule your life. Ask for miracles. Pray for miracles. Join God in the silence of your heart, feel the vibrant force of your being, and from that union allow Christ to live in you the life that He wants to be lived through you. He knows. He loves with perfect love.

20.

The Plain

A message from Jesus, identifying himself as
"the living Christ who lives in you"

I. Prelude

S ons and daughters beloved of the Creator! Here we are, united to you wherever you want to be. There are no limits to our union. Wherever you go, there we are. We are the living expression of the Mother's love, as are you. We have come to dwell with you. We have moved the events of life to be able to spend some time with you.

Remember that you are not alone. You never were and never will be. A multitude of angels and beings of pure love surround you everywhere. We know about your sleeplessness, your worries, and your weariness. We also know of your deep love for your eternal Mother. We know the beauty of your heart.

We want to speak with you once more about the sweetness of love. Everything that comes from God is soft, graceful, and accurate. Love knows nothing of harshness. The subtlety of love is such that only in the silence of the heart can it be savored.

Please close your eyes for a minute or two. Breath deeply. Immerse yourself in the unfathomable abyss of your being. Take my hand, the hand of your eternal friend, the hand of Christ. Begin to immerse yourself more and more in the hollow of the soul, where nothing and nobody unholy can ever enter. Let us enter the depth of your soul where God Herself enjoys you with an inviolable love.

Oh soul of love! Child, drink from the waters of life. Leave the world behind. Leave aside all that worries you. Stay in the solitude of God, where all of creation embraces you lovingly. Come, rest on your beloved's bosom. Enjoy the intimacy of love.

No relationship is more intimate than that which you have with your being. Stay there. Consciously allow the direct relationship with God to be your food.

II. Expression and Feelings

We return once again to expression of feelings. We do it because the fear of feeling has not only made us deny what we feel, but deny the expression of feelings as well.

It is not possible for you to experience freedom if you do not embrace free expression. Drowning your heart is no longer possible. Remember that you are deep into this path of the heart. The transformation has occurred in such a way that you have accessed the perfect knowledge of your being. And with that you have completed the path that led you to truth.

We have come down from the mountaintop. Those who must join us are doing so. They are a multitude. God's work in you is going on day after day, hour after hour. God works in silence. Love does not boast. Life unfolds in silence.

We are showing our sisters and brothers what it means to live in the truth of who we are, just as I did two thousand years ago. We express ourselves as the wisdom of Christ's conscience tells us.

We give a message of encouragement to the fallen if that is what God wants to do through us. We lovingly rebuke if that is what we are called to do. We stay in silence and solitude if the love wants to spend alone time with Her beloved child. We share what we receive free of charge if Christ so disposes. We do nothing without your consent.

Now is a time of silence and solitude for the world. Here we are, you and me, alone in a union of love whose holiness is beyond human words. We are aware of the silence that surrounds us. We are together, united under the stars of a holy night—a night of moon and love, a night of angels singing, a silent night. Just you and me.

Everything that makes sense to you resides in our love relationship. Making yourself aware of our relationship of intimacy is the fullness of your existence. Nothing happens outside of that relationship. Everything that is true is created within our relationship.

You are the repository of all the love that exists in my divine heart. Remember, my child, that there is nothing that my love cannot solve. I am who I am. You are who you are. Ours is a holy relationship.

III. Times of the Holy Relationship

My beloved, the grace of the direct relationship with the living Christ who lives in you has been given you. That is a direct relationship with God. Remember that you are living in times of a new spirituality based on a greater knowledge of God's love, one marked by a direct relationship with God.

Do not worry about the fruits of this relationship. The harvest is abundant. You can already see many of the fruits of our union. You will see many more. Yet they will be almost as nothing compared to the abundance of the fruits of holiness that arise from you because of our union.

Remember that demonstrating the direct relationship that you and I have is your mission. In the measure in which you manifest it, you make it visible; and to that extent you grow in the unity consciousness that we truly are. Unity with everything created resides in what you are. This does not mean that what is outside you need be inside. It means that your nature shares with all being the same essence and substance.

Let the world keep turning. Stay in my arms. Now everything is silent. The birds of the sky are silent. The rivers flow serenely without disturbing the night. All creation sleeps. But our souls melt more deeply. We are growing in union.

We have talked about the expression of feelings. It is necessary. For this, first we travel the path of the silence of the heart. Then we allow being to express itself. The manner in which this expression is realized will vary, given the vastness of what you are. Embrace, sing, dance, cry, moan. Express yourself! But always remember that you and I are one. That nothing can separate you from my love.

Your life is in my hands, literally, in such a way that you have nothing to fear. Fearlessly express yourself in this way or that. Do not make the matter of the expression of feelings into a new doctrine. Simply enjoy being alive with naturalness in every moment.

Remember that the love you need already lives in you, and nowhere else. It was never apart from you. Nobody gave it to you except God in your creation. It is unnecessary to ask for love or to seek love. What a joy to know this! You never suffered because you did not receive love; all pain came from your difficulty giving love.

IV. Expression and Sharing

To express yourself is to give. This simple statement contains a universe of wisdom and truth. It is important that you listen well. Keep these words in the silence of your heart.

The only thing that truly makes sense is love, given. It is true that you were created to be loved, but only to the extent that you first receive the love of God can you give it because of what love is.

From now on I ask you to become aware of the love you give. This love adopts multiple forms. It may be giving company to someone lonely, or tolerating something or someone who was difficult for you. Perhaps it is given in works of solidarity or in simple gestures of caring for a plant or a pet. It does not matter how love is expressed.

Every expression of love is a way to give love. This is why I express my love for you. Each time you allowed love to express itself through you, you felt it in your heart and also in your mind because your mind rested in peace. Each time you expressed your love, in thousands of different ways, you remained in unity.

At the end of life only the love given will remain. This is why I urge you, again and again, to express feelings. And I urge you to express love because only love is real.

You are ready to understand this matter of the expression of feelings and freedom of thought in relation to the practice of the power of silence. The only thing you should express is love and that you can only do from the heart, which is the center of your being. This is because anything other than love is nothing and therefore cannot be shared. Giving is sharing.

Expressing yourself from love, which is what we are talking about, is a way of extending the will of God.

Expression is not itself an act of will. It is a matter of being. There is no possible choice in this. It is the same as saying that there are no neutral thoughts—all produce effects at some level. Those effects are their expression.

Not saying something out of fear, or saying it out of fear, will generate guilt and guilt will be the expression of that fear. Saying something from love or being silent in love creates more love. It is not about expressing or not expressing. In one way or another you always express yourself. Your choice is to express yourself from love or from fear.

What is the fruit of the expression? Knowledge. What is not expressed is hidden. What remains submerged in darkness causes fear, not because it is frightening, but because it cannot be seen in the light.

Nothing need be hidden in God, or in you. There is no need to hide your feelings or thoughts. All are good. All come from your being, so that expressing yourself freely will allow you to know yourself and others to know you.

What we speak of is that you allow the energy of feelings and thoughts to bring you what they come to bring you. You should be aware of the tendency to quickly get rid of emotions or mental processes that you do not like. Do not think that the anger or dislike you feel is sinful. It has something to tell you. Listen to those feelings. Embrace them.

Fear is one of the obstacles to free expression that exists in the patterns of thought and emotional responses. For this reason I have talked so much about it.

21.

The Power of God in You

A message from Jesus, identifying himself as
"the living Christ who lives in you"

I. Being and Power

Holy ones, perfect expressions of God's love! Today I have come to dwell with you who are the presence of love and perfect unity. I come from where the light of truth dwells, a place that is not a place and yet exists, eternally created by the Mother, where only the tenderness of love dwells.

I am one with you here where the truth shines in all its glory. This dimension of existence in which we dwell in unity with God and with your true self is your link with unity.

I am here in response to your call and because of the will of the Creator. I come to reveal even more of the mysteries of Heaven. What a joy it is to discover holy truth. What a joy it is to dwell in your heart and for you to live in mine. I am one and many at the same time. I am everything.

In this session we will speak of power. Every creation of God is clothed in power. There is no impotence, no unconsciousness, and no ignorance. No absence exists with God. God is perfect plenitude.

Feeling powerless has caused you to live submerged in fear. As an individual and as a species, the impotence of the forces of your life has scared you as you tried to survive.

Holy creatures, that is not true life. Living is fullness. The fearful cannot be full because fear prevents the expression of love, and only through love can the fullness of your being be reached. Please listen well now: In you lies the power of God.

Do you not feel helpless? Regardless of whether you would answer "yes" or "no," please follow me in this session because true power is unknown in the world.

Because everything that belongs to God belongs to you, there must be a way for you to reach it. Where does real power reside? How do you get and hold on to it? And why? How do you access your inheritance—the treasures of the Kingdom?

I speak here of how to claim what rightfully belongs to you, your divine inheritance bestowed upon you from the very moment of your creation.

The power of God is the power of love. It exists in the mind and Heart of God, remembering that we no longer distinguish between mind and heart, thought and feeling, since both are the same, an undivided unit, although expressed differently.

II. The Heart of God

God created you in perfect holiness and beauty. She is Creator of all that is true—a being whose intelligence surpasses all human understanding, whose wisdom surpasses all measure, an eternal Father whose authority is beyond the imagination, a divine Mother whose sweetness exceeds the tenderness of all the mothers of the Earth.

God's mind has only thoughts of pure love through which She creates. God also has a heart, the source from which love springs. Her heart is an infinite universe from which everything emerges in perfect peace and holiness. The Sacred Heart of God is an eternal fire of creation without end. It is a creative nucleus of infinite power.

Once again I ask you to extend your imagination far beyond its usual limits. Imagine the most Sacred Heart of the Mother as a sphere of diamond light in whose center burns an eternal fire.

Begin to see with the eyes of spirit how that sphere enlarges more and more until it covers the entire universe. It grows so much that you can no longer distinguish its outline. It is a circle of light with neither beginning nor end. It is the eternal circle of the life of God. Observe how the circle rotates incessantly in an endless rhythmic movement. The fire that burns inside the Heart of God grows, and grows, and grows. It is the fire of the creative passion of the Creator, a fire to which nothing and nobody can get too close. The fire you see is the divine essence. It is the being from which everything arose. It is the burning fire of God's love.

The power that resides in the Heart of God is the only real power. It is a power capable of creating with infinite intelligence the multiple dimensions of creation. Remember that existence is not of a single dimension. The dimension of time and space is only one of the infinite realities created and yet to be created.

What we have called the condensation of fearful conscious-ness, which is what the ego is, is that somehow you made the deliberate decision to disconnect yourself from the power of God. You wanted to be separate.

To move away from love and truth is to distance oneself from God. We already know this clearly. The rest follows. If you separate yourself from love, you separate yourself from the Divine Mind and the Sacred Heart. By doing that, you renounce the power of God in you. Obviously that power is not absent from your mind or heart, but it is reduced to a minimal expression.

On the physical plane you have been using a small fraction of your true mind, a minimum of your mental abilities, such as, to put it in simple terms, ten percent of your abilities.

You are clothed with an immeasurably greater power than you can imagine. Not only can you fly, literally speaking, you can be in more than one place at a time, as well as see all past, present, and future time. You can create dimensions of existence in union with God.

The power that comes from God, as well as everything that emerges from Her, resides in your being. It cannot be anywhere else. As I have said, do not look for happiness, but be happy. In the same way I must now say: do not seek the power of God, but be that power. This means that you become one with Her.

You cannot create the power of God, but you can remain attached to it, just as you can remain attached to love.

Your mind is an extension of the Divine Mind, just as your heart is an extension of the Sacred Heart. If you were not connected with the mind of God you could not think. You literally think with the mind of God or not at all.

If life is thought and you are life, can you then stop thinking? No, you cannot stop thinking, because you would cease to exist. But you can become unaware of the thoughts that God thinks of you. You can block the expression of love through you. In other words, you are free to allow love to be accepted by you and to flow through you.

III. Power and Love

Let us return now to the vision of the diamond sphere with an immense blazing fire within it. This vision is a representation of the power of God, which is the power of love. We cannot speak of power without speaking of love because only love is powerful.

Does it not make sense that God has put power and love together as an inseparable unit? What would happen if the power of God could be used for something other than perfect love?

Ultimately, all fear originates in the fear of the power of God. Fearing God is something that the fearful know very well. We have already spoken of this.

What we are doing now is reconnecting you with your true power. For this, it is necessary that you first recognize it, for what you do not accept with your mind and heart cannot serve what you really are.

Power can be active or potential. It can be manifested or not manifested. The same occurs with love. All power resides in love, therefore in your being.

You are powerful. You have the power to make your mornings be as you wish with all your heart. You have the power to make a whole Heaven. You have the power to work miracles. You have the power to heal bodies and raise the dead. The power that resides in your being can do all this and much more.

Let us examine why you would fear the power of God. You think that if you use that power, it could turn against you because you have had the experience that what you created— your ego—turned against you with all its perversity.

Let us assume for a moment that the power of God can be turned against you. Realize that if that were true, that which would turn against your being is nothing other than the ineffable sweetness of love. The power of God is Her love and vice versa.

You can communicate with us and with the entire universe that lives in love. There is no limit to real communication. You can be aware of other dimensions, as well as the dimension of time and space. Limiting your awareness is an option but it is not God's will for you. The same applies to your abilities.

To reconnect with the power of God you must remain in the presence of love. It is important to understand that there is no question of whether or not you are a bearer of God's power but how to access that power and remain in it eternally. I said the same thing when I spoke of access and permanence in Christ consciousness.

It is in Christ that all power and all glory reside. It is through the living Christ who lives in you that you are as powerful as God in being one with Her. It is in the mind of Christ and your Immaculate Heart that your being and the pure love of God are united with all that is holy, perfect, and beautiful. You will not find power in any place other than in your own being.

Outside of love there is no power possible because outside of love is nothing. Remember, only love is real. Therefore, only the power of love is real.

Creation exists because of the power of love. Her love sustains its existence. Her power creates and recreates eternally. Her wisdom establishes it in an inalterable order. The power of life that you see with the eyes of the body is the power of God manifested in form. Nothing can stop life.

IV. Power and Fear

Fear of the abuse of power engendered in you a mechanism that annulled the awareness of your own power. Certainly the power of love is something you know well.

You have replaced the power of love with the power of anger, which is nothing but fear. That apparent ego power, which is all that you associate with violence, aggression, anger, and many other different forms of fear, is the substitute for love.

Fear seems powerful but is not. Your weakness is evident, and that is what you fear most. Thus you fear fear. In other words, you are not afraid of fear because of its power but because of its weakness. Fear weakens. Accordingly fear has the power to eliminate from your conscious experience the extension of love.

The love of God, which is the only real love and therefore the only reality, does not stop spreading because you do not want to welcome it and allow it to manifest voluntarily through what you are. Love will spread with or without your consent. This must be clarified.

Your consent is one with God's. When you were created you gave your Yes to your Mother and Creator. But concerning the matter of not allowing the extension of love, the consent I refer to is that of your human aspect.

Your divine nature does not block the extension of love or reject the power of God. Your human nature does, but now that will cease because both natures have met in love.

Giving your humanity the power of God is absolutely possible. I proved this when I lived on Earth as a human being, as you do now.

The fear of the power of love is so great that it is buried in your mind and heart, and is the fear of not knowing what to do with power. You think that if you take charge of your power you could use it to harm because that is what you have seen in the world. You know from experience that the powerful of the world almost always use the power they acquired to hurt others, or at least on behalf of their ego—nothing you want.

You created a mechanism that originally came from love but that is far from truth. By this mechanism you annulled the expression of the divine power that lives in you. Ultimately, you think it is better not to be powerful than to succumb to the abuse of power, especially if that power is as great as the power of God.

What would happen if you used God's power for harm? This question is in the pattern of your thinking, even if you do not think much about it. So we must dismantle the erroneous associations that exist in this matter.

The power of love cannot be used. God knows not of use or abuse. Everything that God is—and therefore everything that arises from Her heart—comes from love and is love. Therefore the power of God can only serve the cause of love. It cannot be for anything else.

Holy sons and daughters, you cannot succumb to the abuse of the power of love. You can never love too much. Love is powerful, and has the ability to create whole universes of infinite creations. Remember, everything that surrounds you comes from love and is the power that gives you life.

Once you recognize and accept the absolute inoffensiveness of God's power, you begin to feel comfortable with it as your own power. There is no difference between the power of your being and the power of love because your being is love. Nor is there any difference between the power of God and your power because your Mother and you are one.

If I have demonstrated the power from above, and that that power did not necessarily come from me although it expressed through me, it was so that you could recognize it. I am not more powerful than you, since you and I are one. All power and all glory belong to you forever and ever.

Remain in love and the power of God will do in you and through you what only She knows and can do. You need not manipulate it or know how to use it or what to do with it. You do not need to do anything but recognize and welcome it.

As long as you remain in union consciously, to that extent your feelings of helplessness will fade away. Finally you will recognize that the power of God and the sweetness of love are one and the same, just as you are one and the same with the living Christ who lives in you.

To let the power of God be manifested through you is the same as saying, let yourself be loved. I am calling you to claim your true power, now and forever. Do not worry about how this will come about. In the direct relationship with God all Her power will shine in you. You will know what the power of the Most High is about and you will rest eternally in the security of love.

Final Words

A message from Jesus, identifying himself as "the living Christ who lives in you"

Friend of my soul, holy son or daughter of light! We have reached the end of the fourth book of this work of wisdom and love. We walk together on the path of direct relationship with God.

How much joy it gives us to be one and many, power united to your heart!

The beauty of your being cannot be expressed in human words, nor can the greatness of your heart.

With joy we join you. We are always by your side and always will be. We are one with you. Together we are the eternal reality of love.

We thank you for the time you have dedicated to these words from Heaven. Thank you for answering the call from on High. You have chosen the best part and it shall not be taken from you. You have chosen to follow the voice of truth.

Remember, my voice is like the wind—you know not from whence it comes or where it goes. My voice is a breath of living love, a breeze that carries docile hearts through the flight of freedom of the children of God.

Let us continue with joy and peace. Let us continue playing together the beautiful love game. And with those who were waiting join us, we will proceed on the path of love as the multitude of Christs that we truly are.

I ask you to continue to hold my hand and the hand of your Heavenly Mother. United we will call everyone to come to the feast of love and creation, the feast of Heaven.

Rejoice, you who receive these words. You are the witnesses of the Second Advent. You are the witnesses of God's love. Share these words wherever you are. Go around the world announcing the good news. Christ has arrived. Christ is here.

Blessed are all my children.

A Mystical Relationship

Clarifications by Sebastian Blaksley

I. Relative to Love

D uring the manifestations received, I was given to understand that the work would be composed of one hundred and forty-four sessions, which should be grouped into seven books. I was also informed of the titles of each of them, even before receiving their content. The titles will be, respectively, Echoes of Holiness, Let Yourself Be Loved, Homo-Christus Deo, Wisdom, The Holy Dwelling, The Divine Relationship, and The Way of Being. Each book will consist of twenty-one sessions, with the exception of the seventh which will have eighteen.

There is a numerical relationship whose explanation exceeds the purpose of these writings, but which was shown to me so that it can be understood that in divine creation there is harmony and order in everything. Nothing happens outside the harmonies of Heaven. This order is governed by love, which contains all perfection within itself.

Based on what I received, it is clearly understood that everything exists in relationship. Nothing but love is absolute. Relationship connects all with everything as well as with source.

The relationship of the numbers of books, total sessions, and sessions per book within this work establishes a divine numerical relationship. The numbers themselves are symbols that carry a message from heaven.

II. Christin Incarnated

The one hundred and forty-four sessions are a living expression of "the Redeemed of the Lamb." I was given to understand that this symbol represents the millions of people and beings that on this Earth, in these times, are here incarnating the Christ of God, creating a new Heaven and a new Earth by extending the love of Jesus and Mary, just as the resurrection of Christ has established it from all eternity. They are the preparers of the Second Coming. They are incarnated Christs. Christs are incarnating all over the world, in all religions, contexts, genders, ages, and realms.

With the word "realms" I mean that the incarnation of Christ, which is the miraculous gift of the resurrection, as part of the Second Coming, is not something that only happens in human beings but in all the living kingdoms of the Earth. The Redeemed of the Lamb are not something exclusive to an institution or religious tradition. In fact, it is not related to forms of religion at all, but to spirituality. They are the ones who have consciously made the choice for love. That is why this work is named as it is. I understood this some time after I received the title, which was given to me in a different way from how I receive the manifestations.

The number of sessions in each book, twenty-one, represents and carries within itself a spiritual transformation, which has a rhythm and can only be created as an effect of love. It is also related to pure divine reality. It represents the way of being of the One who created life, who is three times holy, and seven times true.

The number of books, seven, brings the reality of wisdom, of pure thought. It refers the soul to the truth from which it emerges, the pure thought of God.

These numerical relations are somewhat like a rhythm, the timing and silences of music. They allow the whole reach a beauty that can only be created in harmony.

III. Beyond Words

Since the thinking mind is incapable of absorbing the deep meanings of divine truth, it is impossible at the intellectual level to understand the purpose of the structure and content of the sessions and books of the complete work. However, the soul can recognize truth when it makes an appearance, despite the fact that it cannot be put into words. Thus both the content and the way in which these writings have been structured are part of the totality of this manifestation.

The tone, color, and rhythm of the words of this work cause an effect on the heart that is open to receive them for what they are: a letter of love given from Heaven to grow in a greater knowledge of God's love—a gift given with the very love with which it was received.

As you go through each book you can grow in the awareness of the direct relationship with Christ, your true self. In this sense, this work is a journey in which the soul goes hand in hand with love, a journey without distance that begins and ends in the Heart of God.

I hope that these words will lead you to love more, through the return to the first love that is God. Thus they will have fulfilled the purpose from which, for all eternity, they were conceived.

Resources

Further information is available at
www.chooseonlylove.org

Audiobooks of this series narrated in English by Mandi Solk,
and narrated in Spanish by Sebastián Blaksley, are available
on Audible.com, Amazon.com, and on iTunes.

Online conversations about *Choose Only Love* can be found on
Facebook *(Choose Only Love)* and Youtube *(Soplo de amor vivo)*

Edición en español por editorial
Tequisté, www.tequiste.com

Information about the original Spanish-language book,
E*lige solo el amor*, and the companion book *Mi diálogo con
Jesús y María: un retorno al amor* is available at
www.fundacionamorvivo.org

Information about the related work, *Un Curso de Amor*,
is available at www.fundacionamorvivo.org

Other Works from Take Heart Publications

A Course of Love is a living course received from
Jesus by Mari Perron. It leads to the recognition,
through experience, of the truth of who we really are
as human and divine beings—a truth much more
magnificent than we previously could imagine.
For more information go to www.acourseoflove.org.

The Choose Only Love Series

Book One: Echoes of Holiness
Book Two: Let Yourself Be Loved
Book Three: Homo-Christus Deo
Book Four: Wisdom
Book Five: The Holy Dwelling
Book Six: The Divine Relationship
Book Seven: The Way of Being

About the Receiver

Born in 1968, Sebastián Blaksley is a native of Buenos Aires, Argentina, born into a large traditional Catholic family. He attended the Colegio del Salvador, a Jesuit school of which the headmaster was Jorge Bergoglio, the current Pope Francis. Although he wanted to be a monk as a young man, his family did not consider it acceptable, and the inner voice that he always obeyed let him know that: "You must be in the world, without being of the world." He studied Business Administration in Buenos Aires and completed his postgraduate studies in the U.S. He held several highly responsible positions in well-known international corporations, living and working in the U.S., England, China, and Panama. He then founded a corporate consulting firm in Argentina that he led for 10 years. Sebastián has two daughters with his former wife.

At the age of six, Sebastián was involved in a near-fatal accident during which he heard a voice, which later identified itself as Jesus. Ever since he has continued to hear that voice. Sebastián says: "Since I can remember, I have felt the call of Jesus and Mary to live abandoned to their will. I am devoted to my Catholic faith."

In 2013, he began to record messages from his mystical experiences. In 2016 he miraculously discovered *A Course of Love* and felt the call to devote himself to bringing it to the Spanish-speaking world. He also now receives, transcribes, and shares what the voice of Christ—the voice of love—dictates. Most recently he has received *Choose Only Love*, a series of seven books.

Sebastián is president of the nonprofit Fundación Un Curso de Amor, www.fundacionamorvivo.org, through which he shares *A Course of Love*.

Made in the USA
Coppell, TX
04 March 2021